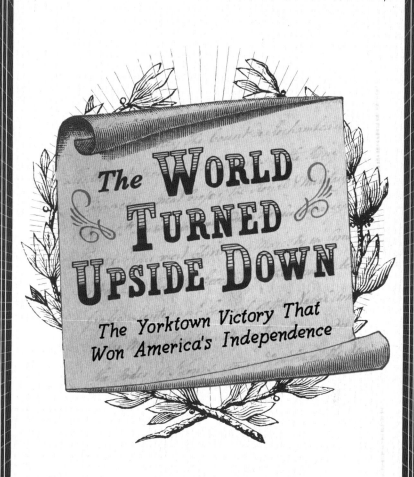

The WORLD TURNED UPSIDE DOWN

The Yorktown Victory That Won America's Independence

by

TIM GROVE

ABRAMS BOOKS FOR YOUNG READERS

NEW YORK

Cataloging-in-Publication Data has been applied for
and may be obtained from the Library of Congress.

ISBN 978-1-4197-4994-0

Text © 2022 Tim Grove
Edited by Howard W. Reeves
Book design by Melissa Jane Barrett

Printed and bound in China
10 9 8 7 6 5 4 3 2 1

ABRAMS The Art of Books
195 Broadway, New York, NY 10007
abramsbooks.com

⋆ CONTENTS ⋆

List of
★ CHARACTERS ★

AMERICANS

GENERAL GEORGE WASHINGTON
commander in chief of the Continental Army

MAJOR GENERAL LAFAYETTE
a French aristocrat and military officer

JAMES
an enslaved man

THOMAS JEFFERSON
Virginia governor, statesman

GENERAL THOMAS NELSON
a general in the Virginia militia and later Virginia governor

LIEUTENANT COLONEL ALEXANDER HAMILTON
a military officer and aide to Washington

LIEUTENANT COLONEL JOHN LAURENS
a military officer and aide to Washington

BRITISH

GENERAL SIR HENRY CLINTON
commander of all forces in North America

GENERAL LORD CHARLES CORNWALLIS
top British commander in Virginia

BRIGADIER GENERAL BENEDICT ARNOLD
former American military commander

LIEUTENANT COLONEL BANASTRE TARLETON
cavalry officer under Cornwallis

REAR ADMIRAL THOMAS GRAVES
Royal Navy commander in the Second Battle of the Capes

BRIGADIER GENERAL CHARLES O'HARA
second-in-command under Cornwallis

MAJOR GENERAL WILLIAM PHILLIPS
military commander in Virginia

ADMIRAL MARRIOT ARBUTHNOT
Royal Navy commander in the First Battle of the Capes

FRENCH

JEAN-BAPTISTE-DONATIEN DE VIMEUR, COMTE DE ROCHAMBEAU
commander of French ground forces in North America

FRANÇOIS JOSEPH PAUL, COMTE DE GRASSE
commander of the French navy

CHARLES RENÉ DOMINIQUE SOCHET, CHEVALIER DESTOUCHES
naval commander in the First Battle of the Capes

JACQUES-MELCHIOR SAINT LAURENT, COMTE DE BARRAS
naval commander based in Newport, Rhode Island

MAIN DIARISTS

BARON LUDWIG VON CLOSEN
a nobleman from Bavaria (in present-day Germany) who served as an aide to Rochambeau

LIEUTENANT EBENEZER DENNY
a twenty-year-old soldier in a Pennsylvania regiment

CAPTAIN JOHANN VON EWALD
a Hessian (German) military officer who fought with the British

LOUIS-FRANÇOIS-BERTRAND DU PONT D'AUBEVOYE, COMTE DE LAUBERDIÈRE
a twenty-one-year-old aide and translator for General Rochambeau in the French army

JOSEPH PLUMB MARTIN
a young private in his teens who fought for the Continental Army

DR. JAMES THACHER
an army surgeon from Massachusetts who served with the Continental Army

ST. GEORGE TUCKER
a major in the Virginia militia, translator for Governor and General Thomas Nelson

★ PREFACE ★

EVERYTHING THAT HAPPENED IN THIS BOOK is true, and all the characters were real people. The book is based on historical evidence. Historians try to put a puzzle together from the many pieces of historical evidence they find while doing research; sometimes there are pieces missing. Fortunately, quite a few diaries and official papers are available to provide firsthand accounts of the American Revolution.

The United States owes a great debt of gratitude to France. Simply put, without French help during the American Revolution, the United States would probably not have achieved independence. This book tells the story of people from very different backgrounds who worked together toward a common goal. Others worked hard to stop them. Every historical event can be viewed from multiple perspectives, and that makes history fascinating.

Why are so few women's perspectives included in this book? This tale relies on available historical sources. As it focuses on the military events that led up to the Siege of Yorktown, and because women in the eighteenth century did not play a role in warfare, there are no known records kept by women about military tactics and outcomes. Further, they did not hold many positions of leadership that might have been documented. I've woven women's perspectives into the story whenever relevant and possible.

In a war, there are many different types of military units. When the American Revolution began, the United States did not exist,

so no professional army existed. Each colony was responsible for its own protection or received aid from British troops. When fighting erupted, the various colonies responded to a call for soldiers by sending their own regiments, which joined together to become the Continental Army under General George Washington. Each colony also formed militias, usually based in a county, that stayed in the colony to defend it. Militia soldiers were usually part-time soldiers.

In our day of instant communication, it is very difficult to grasp the incredibly slow speed of communication in the eighteenth century. Think about life with no telephone, email, texts, instant messaging, TV, or radio. The challenges for military commanders spread over hundreds of miles meant they had to trust one another to make good decisions; often their correspondence crossed in delivery, meaning an answer they received could be referring to a question they asked several letters before. Whenever possible, they preferred to send communication by water transportation, as it was faster due to the poor state of roads at the time.

Finally, a few notes about terminology and spellings: In America, Lafayette became known by his last name though it was spelled in different ways. Marquis was a title he inherited when his father died. In the eighteenth century and until the mid-twentieth century, the term "negro" was used in common language to describe someone with dark skin. Negro is the Spanish word for "black."

Today it is considered a dated, offensive term by many people. I have used the word only in direct quotations from the period. Also, Yorktown, Virginia, was referred to as "York" or "little York" in 1781.

This book tells the story of the struggle for freedom. But freedom means different things to the different characters. James Lafayette wants freedom to make his own decisions in life, something denied to him as an enslaved person. Leaders like George Washington and Thomas Jefferson want a free society with a government representing its citizens. And yet, as slave owners, they deny freedom and citizenship to enslaved people. General Washington fights for freedom for many and denies freedom to others. Is it possible to be a strong military leader and enslave people at the same time? Yes. Does one excuse or cancel the other? No. History is complicated because people are complicated.

✫ INTRODUCTION ✫

This print of the Battle of Lexington shows British troops firing on the militia. The artist, Amos Doolittle, engraved it in 1775 after touring the battlefield.

AS THE FIRST LIGHT OF DAWN COLORED THE sky, a small band of defiant farmers and artisans stood blocking a regiment of British soldiers clad in red uniforms. It was an April morning in 1775, and the place was the village green of Lexington, Massachusetts. The British were headed west from their base in Boston to Concord, to raid the military arsenal where weapons were stored. The colonial militia was not going to let that happen. Its leaders had decided that now was the time to make a stand. In the tension of the moment, a shot ripped through the still air. A sudden exchange of gunfire left eight militiamen dead on the grass. To this day, no one knows who fired that first shot. It has often been called "the shot heard round the world," because that moment became the point of no return. People were willing to die for something they believed, and the American Revolution had begun.

The Battles of Lexington and Concord that day put the mighty world power of Great Britain on notice that the colonists would pay the ultimate price to be free from King George III's rule. Britain's unfair trade and tax policies could not continue. What started in a small Massachusetts town would six years later come to a big conclusion in a small Virginia town named York.

Each of the thirteen British colonies spread down the eastern coast of North America had an individual government that made its own laws, under the authority of King George. The previous year, 1774, the colonies had sent representatives to Philadelphia to discuss the challenges they all faced with the British government. This meeting was called the First Continental Congress, and its members agreed to a unified boycott of British goods. They also voted to meet again the following year if Parliament, the British government in London, did not address their grievances. After the bloodshed at Lexington and Concord, the Second Continental Congress met and recognized the need to unite behind Massachusetts in the effort against Britain. It was a bold move because as a whole, the thirteen colonies

King George III of Great Britain was thirty-seven years old in 1775 and had been king for fifteen years. This painting was completed four years before the start of the American Revolution.

In this portrait, General George Washington wears the light blue sash of commander in chief. Artist Charles Willson Peale painted it in 1776 just before Congress issued the Declaration of Independence.

had no common standing army (only their own militias to be called upon if needed), no common navy, no banks, no financial income, no strong military leaders, and no central leadership. They didn't even have a flag. The population was not united either. At least 20 percent of the citizens did not want to cut ties with Great Britain; they would remain loyal, and were called loyalists. Those fighting for justice saw themselves as patriots, but to British authorities, the agitators were unlawful rebels.

Congress realized it needed to appoint a person to lead the combined military efforts. It voted unanimously to put the country's fate in the hands of a man from Virginia named George Washington. In many ways, Washington was not an obvious choice to lead the American military forces. A Virginia farmer and surveyor, he had gained military experience two decades earlier fighting alongside the British on the frontier during the French and Indian War (1754–63). Yet, unlike the top British commanders he would be fighting against this time, Washington had never commanded more than a handful of men. He had not been schooled in the tactics and strategy of war. He had never won a major battle! Now he faced one of the toughest military forces in the world. Well aware of his inexperience, Washington admitted as much when he accepted the position. Standing before Congress in June 1775, he said, "I beg it be remembered by every Gentleman in this room, that I this day declare with the utmost sincerity, I do not think myself equal to the command I am honored with."

Washington traveled to Boston and assumed his position on July 3, 1775. He began the tasks of setting up a Continental Army

IN CONGRESS, JULY 4, 1776.

A DECLARATION

BY THE REPRESENTATIVES OF THE

UNITED STATES OF AMERICA,

IN GENERAL CONGRESS ASSEMBLED.

WHEN in the Course of human Events, it becomes necessary for one People to dissolve the Political Bands which have connected them with another, and to assume among the Powers of the Earth, the separate and equal Station to which the Laws of Nature and of Nature's God entitle them, a decent Respect to the Opinions of Mankind requires that they should declare the causes which impel them to the Separation.

We hold these Truths to be self-evident, that all Men are created equal, that they are endowed by their Creator with certain unalienable Rights, that among these are Life, Liberty, and the Pursuit of Happiness—That to secure these Rights, Governments are instituted among Men, deriving their just Powers from the Consent of the Governed, that whenever any Form of Government becomes destructive of these Ends, it is the Right of the People to alter or to abolish it, and to institute new Government, laying its Foundation on such Principles, and organizing its Powers in such Form, as to them shall seem most likely to effect their Safety and Happiness. Prudence, indeed, will dictate that Governments long established should not be changed for light and transient Causes; and accordingly all Experience hath shewn, that Mankind are more disposed to suffer, while Evils are sufferable, than to right themselves by abolishing the Forms to which they are accustomed. But when a long Train of Abuses and Usurpations, pursuing invariably the same Object, evinces a Design to reduce them under absolute Despotism, it is their Right, it is their Duty, to throw off such Government, and to provide new Guards for their future Security. Such has been the patient Sufferance of these Colonies; and such is now the Necessity which constrains them to alter their former Systems of Government. The History of the present King of Great-Britain is a History of repeated Injuries and Usurpations, all having in direct Object the Establishment of an absolute Tyranny over these States. To prove this, let Facts be submitted to a candid World.

He has refused his Assent to Laws, the most wholesome and necessary for the public Good.

He has forbidden his Governors to pass Laws of immediate and pressing Importance, unless suspended in their Operation till his Assent should be obtained; and when so suspended, he has utterly neglected to attend to them.

He has refused to pass other Laws for the Accommodation of large Districts of People, unless those People would relinquish the Right of Representation in the Legislature, a Right inestimable to them, and formidable to Tyrants only.

He has called together Legislative Bodies at Places unusual, uncomfortable, and distant from the Depository of their public Records, for the sole Purpose of fatiguing them into Compliance with his Measures.

He has dissolved Representative Houses repeatedly, for opposing with manly Firmness his Invasions on the Rights of the People.

He has refused for a long Time, after such Dissolutions, to cause others to be elected; whereby the Legislative Powers, incapable of Annihilation, have returned to the People at large for their exercise; the State remaining in the mean time exposed to all the Dangers of Invasion from without, and Convulsions within.

He has endeavoured to prevent the Population of these States; for that Purpose obstructing the Laws for Naturalization of Foreigners; refusing to pass others to encourage their Migrations hither, and raising the Conditions of new Appropriations of Lands.

He has obstructed the Administration of Justice, by refusing his Assent to Laws for establishing Judiciary Powers.

He has made Judges dependent on his Will alone, for the Tenure of their Offices, and the Amount and Payment of their Salaries.

He has erected a Multitude of new Offices, and sent hither Swarms of Officers to harrass our People, and eat out their Substance.

He has kept among us, in Times of Peace, Standing Armies, without the consent of our Legislatures.

He has affected to render the Military independent of and superior to the Civil Power.

He has combined with others to subject us to a Jurisdiction foreign to our Constitution, and unacknowledged by our Laws; giving his Assent to their Acts of pretended Legislation:

For quartering large Bodies of Armed Troops among us:

For protecting them, by a mock Trial, from Punishment for any Murders which they should commit on the Inhabitants of these States:

For cutting off our Trade with all Parts of the World:

For imposing Taxes on us without our Consent:

For depriving us, in many Cases, of the Benefits of Trial by Jury:

For transporting us beyond Seas to be tried for pretended Offences:

For abolishing the free System of English Laws in a neighbouring Province, establishing therein an arbitrary Government, and enlarging its Boundaries, so as to render it at once an Example and fit Instrument for introducing the same absolute Rule into these Colonies:

For taking away our Charters, abolishing our most valuable Laws, and altering fundamentally the Forms of our Governments:

For suspending our own Legislatures, and declaring themselves invested with Power to legislate for us in all Cases whatsoever.

He has abdicated Government here, by declaring us out of his Protection and waging War against us.

He has plundered our Seas, ravaged our Coasts, burnt our Towns, and destroyed the Lives of our People.

He is, at this Time, transporting large Armies of foreign Mercenaries to compleat the Works of Death, Desolation, and Tyranny, already begun with circumstances of Cruelty and Perfidy, scarcely paralleled in the most barbarous Ages, and totally unworthy the Head of a civilized Nation.

He has constrained our fellow Citizens taken Captive on the high Seas to bear Arms against their Country, to become the Executioners of their Friends and Brethren, or to fall themselves by their Hands.

He has excited domestic Insurrections amongst us, and has endeavoured to bring on the Inhabitants of our Frontiers, the merciless Indian Savages, whose known Rule of Warfare, is an undistinguished Destruction, of all Ages, Sexes and Conditions.

In every stage of these Oppressions we have Petitioned for Redress in the most humble Terms: Our repeated Petitions have been answered only by repeated Injury. A Prince, whose Character is thus marked by every act which may define a Tyrant, is unfit to be the Ruler of a free People.

Nor have we been wanting in Attentions to our British Brethren. We have warned them from Time to Time of Attempts by their Legislature to extend an unwarrantable Jurisdiction over us. We have reminded them of the Circumstances of our Emigration and Settlement here. We have appealed to their native Justice and Magnanimity, and we have conjured them by the Ties of our common Kindred to disavow these Usurpations, which, would inevitably interrupt our Connections and Correspondence. They too have been deaf to the Voice of Justice and of Consanguinity. We must, therefore, acquiesce in the Necessity, which denounces our Separation, and hold them, as we hold the rest of Mankind, Enemies in War, in Peace, Friends.

We, therefore, the Representatives of the UNITED STATES OF AMERICA, in GENERAL CONGRESS, Assembled, appealing to the Supreme Judge of the World for the Rectitude of our Intentions, do, in the Name, and by Authority of the good People of these Colonies, solemnly Publish and Declare, That these United Colonies are, and of Right ought to be, FREE AND INDEPENDENT STATES; that they are absolved from all Allegiance to the British Crown, and that all political Connection between them and the State of Great-Britain, is and ought to be totally dissolved; and that as FREE AND INDEPENDENT STATES, they have full Power to levy War, conclude Peace, contract Alliances, establish Commerce, and to do all other Acts and Things which INDEPENDENT STATES may of right do. And for the support of this Declaration, with a firm Reliance on the Protection of divine Providence, we mutually pledge to each other our Lives, our Fortunes, and our sacred Honor.

Signed by ORDER and in BEHALF of the CONGRESS,

JOHN HANCOCK, PRESIDENT.

ATTEST.
CHARLES THOMSON, SECRETARY.

PHILADELPHIA: PRINTED BY JOHN DUNLAP.

The Declaration of Independence was first published on the evening of July 4, 1776.

made up of men from all the colonies, finding qualified officers, training soldiers, and developing a strategy for fighting the British. Surrounded by patriot soldiers in Boston, the main British army soon evacuated. Washington chased it to New York, where, despite his best efforts, the British eventually attacked and occupied Manhattan in New York City.

One by one, the thirteen colonial governments began voting to separate from Britain. In Congress, the delegates from Virginia proposed a national independence. Congress debated the topic, and on July 4, 1776, it became official. The Continental Congress declared: "That these United Colonies are, and of Right ought to be Free and independent States; that they are Absolved from all Allegiance to the British Crown, and that all political connections between them and the State of Great Britain, is and ought to be totally dissolved."

It was one thing to declare the birth of a new country, quite another to make it happen against a world power that opposed it.

Chapter

1

A New Major General

When word got out that the thirteen colonies were in rebellion, the people of France could not have been happier. France and Great Britain were age-old enemies. A war between them would no sooner end than another one would quickly erupt. From the war's beginning, Congress had hoped that France would become an ally that would contribute not only much-needed funds and weapons but also soldiers and ships. However, France was not prepared for another war at the moment, and it had to tread carefully so that it would not get involved. In the French and Indian War, the previous war in North America, which ended in 1763, France had lost to Britain, and as a result had lost claim to its lands in Canada and between the Appalachian Mountains and the Mississippi River. It would be watching very carefully to see what happened.

In March 1776, Congress had sent Silas Deane, a merchant from Connecticut, as a secret diplomat to Paris. It hoped Deane would be able to negotiate financial aid from the French government. He also began recruiting the services of European soldiers to help train and lead American troops.

Europe had a long history of standing armies, paid professionals trained and ready to fight for Crown and country. Many European officers, and especially French ones, saw the new war in North America as an opportunity to gain military experience and glory. A constant stream of these men, some well qualified, others exaggerating their qualifications, began to contact Deane, who offered them commissions and sent them to Philadelphia. Congress soon grew weary of the many unqualified men who came expecting positions. General Washington in particular became outraged and disgusted with the demanding attitudes of these men and protested: "The distress I am . . . laid under by the application of French officers for commission in our service . . . they are coming in swarms from old France and the Islands." Washington asked Congress what he was expected to do with the foreign men it was commissioning as officers. "These men have no attachment nor ties to the country . . . and are ignorant of the language they are to receive and give orders in . . . and our officers think it exceedingly hard . . . to have strangers put over them, whose merit perhaps is not equal to their own."

Congress finally listened and by mid-1777 had stopped hiring these men. But Deane asked Congress to make one last exception: The Marquis de Lafayette, "a young nobleman of great family connections here [in France] and great wealth is gone to America in a ship of his own, accompanied by some officers of distinction, in order to serve in our armies. He is exceedingly beloved and everybody's good wishes attend him."

Soon thereafter, on a hot July day, a group of exhausted strangers arrived in Philadelphia. The war had been going on for two years, and the Americans were losing. Only one of the men spoke decent English. They had spent thirty-two days traveling seven hundred miles over rough roads, through abominable heat, from Charles Town (present-day Charleston), South Carolina, where their ship had docked. The group had departed that city in splendid carriages, but as one wrote, "four days later our carriages were reduced to splinters. Several of the horses were old and unsteady, and were either worn out or

The Pennsylvania State House, later called Independence Hall, is where
Congress met during much of the American Revolution. In a room on
the lower level, Congress debated and signed both the Declaration of
Independence and the United States Constitution.

lame. We had to leave a part of our luggage behind, and part of
it was stolen. We traveled a great part of the way on foot, often
sleeping in the woods, almost dead with hunger, exhausted by
the heat, several of us suffering from fever and dysentery." It
was their first visit to America. The leader of the little expedition wrote, "The farther I advance north, the better pleased I
am with the country and its people. They refuse me no kindness
or attention, even though most hardly know who I am." He was
on a personal quest: "When I felt American soil under my feet
for the first time . . . my first words were an oath to conquer or
die for America's cause."

The travelers walked directly to the Pennsylvania State House,
where the Continental Congress was meeting. These Frenchmen,
like others before them, carried letters of recommendation and
commissions from Congress's own representatives in Paris. Both

the doorkeeper and a member of Congress read their papers but refused entry. Why this treatment? The group's leader was heart-broken. He decided to write a petition directly to the president of Congress, John Hancock. "After the sacrifices I have made in this cause, I have the right to exact two favors: one is to serve at my own expense—the other is, to serve at first as a volunteer." To stress his zeal, he borrowed words from the Declaration of Independence, pledging his life, his fortune, and his sacred honor to American independence.

Hancock soon realized that the nineteen-year-old making the petition was none other than the Marquis de Lafayette, the same person Deane had said should be the exception. He was one of the wealthiest men in France, with direct access to the French king, and Congress desperately needed France as an ally in the cause of independence. They offered Lafayette a deal: He would receive no pay or compensation of any kind, his rank would be strictly honorary, and he would receive no command or promise of one. But he could join the fight.

On July 31, 1777, Congress passed a resolution stating: "Whereas the Marquis de La Fayette, out of his great zeal to the cause of liberty, in which the United States are engaged, has left his family and connections, and at his own expense come over to offer his services to the United States without pension or particular allowance, and is anxious to risk his life in our cause—Resolved, That his service be accepted, and that in con-sideration of his zeal, illustrious family and connections he have the rank and commission of Major General in the Army of the United States."

This teenager who put on a major general's sash would become one of the most famous soldiers of the American Revolution and

The Marquis de Lafayette, painted a few years after Yorktown by an unidentified French artist, standing in front of a military encampment. He has tied his powdered hair in the popular style of the day, a queue or braid of hair down the back, and he holds a sword in his right hand.

one of the greatest friends of America. Every person in the nation would one day know the name Lafayette.

Marie-Joseph-Paul-Yves-Roch-Gilbert du Motier de La Fayette, his full name, was a French nobleman from a family of warriors that stretched back centuries. He was born in a big stone château, built on the ruins of an old castle, and had grown up hearing stories of knights going off to battle and other "tales of war and glory, in a family so closely tied to memories and sorrows associated with war." His grandfather was wounded three times in battle against the English. British forces had killed his father in battle when Lafayette was only two years old. His mother died when he was twelve, leaving him an inheritance that made him one of the richest people in France.

At age thirteen, he began his military career, entering service in the King's Musketeers, a prestigious company. He trained at the royal riding school at Versailles, where the king's three grandsons were his classmates. When Lafayette married at age seventeen into another noble French family, the royal family attended his wedding reception. He had grown up with the new king, Louis XVI, one of the most powerful men in the world, and could visit the royal palace at Versailles and request an audience with the king, or his queen, Marie Antoinette, at any time. Lafayette had strolled Versailles's lavish gardens and attended glittering balls and receptions in large rooms with richly painted ceilings and gold-encrusted furniture.

What was apparent to everyone was Lafayette's passion for the American cause. He was driven by a fire within to fight for justice. Not satisfied to live a life of ease, Lafayette had read about the Americans' desire for freedom. At a dinner party in France, he had met the British king George III's younger brother, the

Lafayette (*left*) enjoyed a good relationship with King Louis XVI and Queen Marie Antoinette.

Duke of Gloucester. The duke had praised the Americans' love of liberty and inspired Lafayette. He could not stop thinking about the struggle across the Atlantic Ocean. It was an opportunity to avenge France's loss in the recent war with Britain and his father's death, as well as a chance to gain military experience and glory fighting for a cause he believed in. He decided to enlist. There was only one problem: He was a French soldier. Lafayette's planning had to remain secret because he was going against his king's wishes. Louis XVI had forbidden military officers to fight for the American colonists. The king was worried that their involvement would make it look like France was siding with America and would provoke Britain.

While secretly planning his travel to America, Lafayette made an already scheduled trip to Great Britain. "I could not refuse to go without risking the discovery of my secret, and by consenting to take this journey I knew I could better conceal my preparations for a greater one." He visited the French ambassador in London, a relative through his wife, where he was presented to King George III and was the guest of honor at a ball given by Lord George Germaine, British secretary for the American colonies. While attending the opera, he chatted with General Sir Henry Clinton, a future major player in the British fight for America. Many years later, Lafayette wrote about the trip: "A youth of nineteen may be perhaps, too fond of playing a trick upon the king he is going to fight with. But, while I concealed my intentions, I openly avowed my sentiments. I often defended the Americans."

Back in France, Lafayette secured a ship, and he assured his comrades that he had received his family's approval and his wife Adrienne's blessing. He lied. He had not said goodbye to his pregnant wife and infant daughter, and only informed his father-in-law with a letter once he was gone. Adrienne finally received a letter from him six months after his departure. Lafayette and his comrades ended up causing a minor scandal in France by disobeying the French king's orders. They had raced to the French coast and boarded Lafayette's ship, using disguises to elude arrest by the king's troops. His actions threatened great damage to the family name, emotional distress to his young wife, and embarrassment to the French government in its diplomatic relations with Britain. As one of his comrades wrote, "It is certain that this folly will cost him dearly. But if it be said that he has done a foolish thing, it may be answered that he acted from the most honorable motives and that he can hold up his head before all high-minded men."

☆ ☆ ☆

If General Washington was annoyed at Congress's decision regarding Lafayette, adding yet another French officer to his army, he didn't show it. The two men met at a dinner in Philadelphia. Lafayette was in awe of the American leader, a tall warrior not unlike how he imagined his own father and only one year younger. He recalled later that Washington complimented him for his "zeal and sacrifice in coming to America . . . in the most friendly manner, he invited me to reside in his house. I would have the happiness of living in the general quarters of the commander-in-chief as a member of his military family, which offer I accepted with the same sincerity with which it was made." Washington warned that he "could not promise the luxuries of a king's court, but now that Lafayette had become an American soldier, he would undoubtedly adapt with good grace to the hardships of life in a republican army."

A week later, a grateful Lafayette sent a thank-you note to John Hancock. It read, "I wish to serve near the person of General Washington till such time as he may think proper to entrust me with a division of the Army." Lafayette's eyes remained on the prize of military glory.

And so, Lafayette had gone from the mirrored corridors of Versailles to help Americans fight for freedom against Britain. He now served alongside one of the most powerful men in America. He immediately hired two of his fellow travelers as aides, at his own expense. Congress commissioned another of his group but turned away the others, who returned to France. Lafayette had no war experience. Despite his important connections in France, he would need to earn respect in America.

CHAPTER

AUTUMN OF DISAPPOINTMENT

General George Washington had never expected the war to drag on so long. By mid-1780, five years from the first shots, his armies had suffered some major losses and had won some surprising victories. After evacuating Boston, the British had made New York City their headquarters; Washington's troops encamped nearby across the Hudson River, too outnumbered to risk an attack. For nine months, the British also had occupied Philadelphia, forcing Congress to flee west. Shortages of supplies and manpower were constant challenges. In the South, the patriots had suffered a devastating loss when the British army attacked and occupied Charles Town, South Carolina, in the spring of 1780. A British army under General Lord Charles Cornwallis, now in North Carolina, had been gaining ground in an effort to subdue the Southern states. Washington, usually an eternal optimist, was discouraged.

Lafayette watched and learned. As he had told Washington when they first met, "It is to learn and not teach, that I have come." Something about the young man endeared him to Washington. Shortly after joining the American army, he had rushed into action at the Battle of Brandywine, was wounded, and proved his willingness to lead soldiers. Over time, his and Washington's relationship deepened, and a bond of mutual admiration developed. Washington grew to trust and respect Lafayette and to treat him in some ways like the son he never had. Little by little, he gave Lafayette more responsibility. While the marquis originally had come to America on his own, not officially representing

Three American representatives signed the Treaty of Alliance with France in February 1778, including statesman Benjamin Franklin, who was very popular in France.

the French court, Lafayette's "illustrious and important connections," as Washington called them, would prove useful.

America needed to show France that it was serious about gaining independence. A key American victory at Saratoga, in upstate New York, in autumn 1777 finally convinced France that the upstart Americans might just have what it takes to win their freedom. France officially recognized the country of the United States, and the two countries signed a treaty of amity and trade. Supporting the Americans against Great Britain meant that King Louis XVI was condoning people declaring their independence from royal rule; rebelling against their own king. The irony of the French king recognizing America's independence was not lost on most people, especially Lafayette.

What motivated France? It is hard to imagine two more different allies: one ruled by a king, an absolute monarch; the other led by a group of people fighting for independence from their

Created in 1782, this print portrays a lion, representing Great Britain, confronting a snake (the United States), a rooster (France), and two dogs (Spain and Holland) during the American Revolution. The lion says, "You shall all have an old English drubbing to make you quiet."

king and his representative government. They held no common financial or territorial interests or even shared ideals; France had no sympathy for republican ideas. King Louis XVI wanted to weaken Britain, his country's long-standing enemy, and to equalize the balance of power in the world.

But, thus far in the war, the French had only dashed America's hopes. While they had sent gunpowder, arms, cannons, and money, large French military forces never materialized. Brief visits by a small French naval force in Newport, Rhode Island, and Savannah, Georgia, had not advanced the war effort. Washington desperately needed both French troops and the French navy. What would it take to get the French military more involved? Lafayette!

Abigail Adams was married to statesman and second US President John Adams. They lived in Massachusetts. In a letter to her son in France in December 1778, she wrote that Lafayette "is much esteemed" in America.

In 1779, with Washington's blessing, Lafayette returned to France to see if he could influence the king. He was unsure how he would be received since he had left France a fugitive, with a warrant out for his arrest for defying the king's orders. But word of his bravery in America had reached home. He had demonstrated his courage and warrior spirit. The king's cannons roared their welcome. After a brief period of house arrest as a punishment for going against the royal orders, Lafayette made his way to Louis XVI at Versailles.

Teaming up with Congress's

representatives to France, Benjamin Franklin and John Adams, Lafayette secured a promise of new aid for the patriot cause. He returned to America the following year, and Abigail Adams, the wife of John Adams, described the scene in a letter to her husband: "Last week arrived at Boston the Marquis de la Fayette to the universal joy of all who know the Merit and Worth of that Nobleman. He was received with the ringing of Bells, fireing of cannon, bon fires &c." Lafayette brought the good news that seven ships of the line, the largest ships in the navy, carrying ten thousand to twelve thousand troops and chests of coins were on their way across the ocean. Washington was relieved but cautious. He would believe Lafayette's news if the troops and funds arrived.

On July 10, 1780, a forest of sails appeared in the shimmering waters of Narragansett Bay off Newport, Rhode Island. The French had arrived! The commander, General Jean-Baptiste-Donatien de Vimeur, comte de Rochambeau, immediately wrote to Washington, "We are now, sir, under your command." This gesture of service was meant to put Washington's mind at ease and convey the desire to work together.

Washington sent Lafayette to welcome the commander in chief of the French armies in North America. To Rochambeau, Washington wrote of Lafayette: "I have the greatest confidence in him . . . he knows all the circumstances of our army and the country at large; all the information he gives and all the propositions he makes, I entreat you will consider as coming from me." Upon his arrival in Newport, Lafayette eagerly sought out his friends from his French military days, and others he knew. But he soon realized that there was a problem.

Instead of the ten thousand or more troops promised, only five thousand arrived, and thousands of them were not healthy

This painting shows Comte de Rochambeau in his older years. Rochambeau, a highly experienced soldier, was anticipating retirement from the military when he was unexpectedly sent to America.

enough for action. Almost thirteen hundred sailors were also ill. And where were the arms and ammunition also promised? The combined forces would still not be enough for superiority over the British on land or sea. Washington wanted to attack New York or Charles Town, but it would be unwise given these numbers.

To add to the urgency, Washington was at risk of losing much of his own army because enlistments (the amount of time soldiers agreed to serve in the army) would soon be up, and many soldiers would return to their homes.

Frustrated and furious, Lafayette was not as delicate as he could have been. He went so far as to imply that the position of the French at Rhode Island was of no use to the Americans. He forgot the respect expected from a junior officer. Rochambeau had served thirty-seven years in the military and was insulted by his young, inexperienced countryman, who was younger than Rochambeau's own son. At first, he refused to speak more with Lafayette and requested to speak only with Washington, who was not there.

Lafayette knew he had made a mistake. He swallowed his pride and wrote a personal letter full of the praise a French commander would expect from a subordinate. "Permit me to address myself to you with the frankness born of the warm affection I have felt, and endeavored to show you, from my earliest youth . . . If I have offended you, I ask your pardon, for two reasons; first, because I am sincerely attached to you; and secondly, because it is my earnest wish to do everything I can to please you here." His sincerity worked.

With differences smoothed over, Lafayette returned to Washington. The commanding general had learned he must deal directly with his French counterpart. He also bowed to Rochambeau's desire to stay put at Newport, more than two hundred miles from the main Continental Army, to await additional French ships and soldiers. Ultimately, he swallowed this new disappointment. He was forced to delay an attack yet again.

CHAPTER

3

FIRST MEETING

In mid-September 1780, Washington decided it was finally time to pay Rochambeau the personal visit that the French leader had been requesting. He and his contingent set off on horseback from their encampment in Peekskill, New York, on the Hudson River. The group included Lafayette and a young aide in his twenties, Colonel Alexander Hamilton, who spoke French and could

The white silk flag of Washington's Life Guard unit featured the motto "Conquer or Die" and portrayed a guard member holding a horse and receiving a flag from a woman representing "Liberty."

help translate. Hamilton had come to New York from the British West Indies to attend university, and when the war began, he joined a militia unit. He had seen combat in several battles and was always looking for opportunities to increase his status in life. While Hamilton longed for glory in battle, when Washington offered him a position on his staff, the young man could not refuse. He earned Washington's trust as someone in the inner circle. He and Lafayette were close friends, along with another aide, South Carolinian John Laurens. As Washington's aides, they shared living and office quarters and developed a sense of brotherhood.

The Commander-in-Chief's Guard, more often called the Life Guard, served as Washington's security detail and surrounded him at all times. The Life Guard was an elite unit easily identified by

Alexander Hamilton served as an aide to General Washington for four years during the American Revolution. This painting was completed about ten years after Yorktown when he was serving in the new United States government as the first secretary of the Treasury.

the members' distinctive uniforms. They wore buff-and-blue coats, and their leather hats featured a white plume with a blue tip and a bearskin crest. Comprising a captain and fifty men, the best from each of the thirteen states, they had formed early in the war with the sole responsibility of protecting Washington. He never knew when the enemy might try to kidnap or harm him.

John Laurens probably commissioned this miniature portrait of himself in Philadelphia a year before Yorktown. A miniature is a very detailed and very small painting that one can carry with them. This was painted by notable American artist Charles Willson Peale.

Rather than take the time to travel the long journey to Newport, the Americans and French agreed to meet halfway at Hartford, in Connecticut. Washington was an experienced horseman and often rode long distances on horseback. His favorite horse, Nelson, was his preferred mount. Nelson was reddish brown with a white face and legs. The party crossed wooded hills and the Housatonic and Naugatuck Rivers, traveling through small towns (including one named for Washington), finally reaching Hartford in the center of the state. This area was strongly patriotic, and cannons boomed a greeting to the commander in chief.

Both sides were curious to meet their allies. Rochambeau would report directly to Washington and had heard so many opinions about the man. Washington wasted no time in charming the French. His very presence commanded attention. At six feet, two inches tall, he towered over most men.

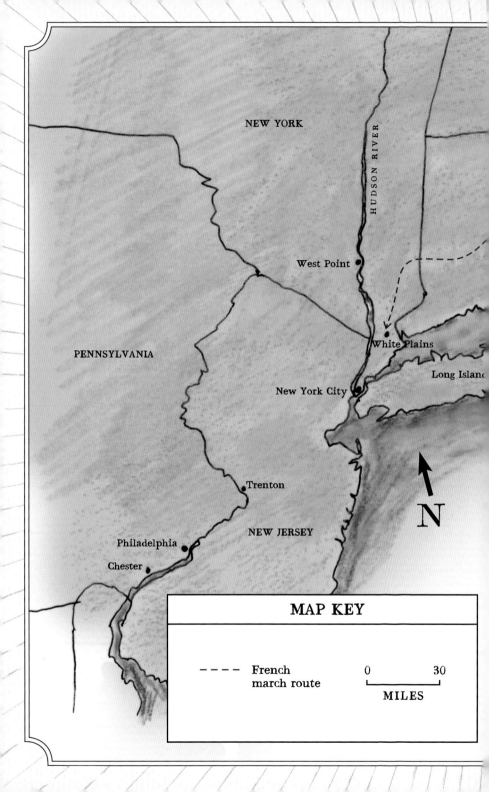

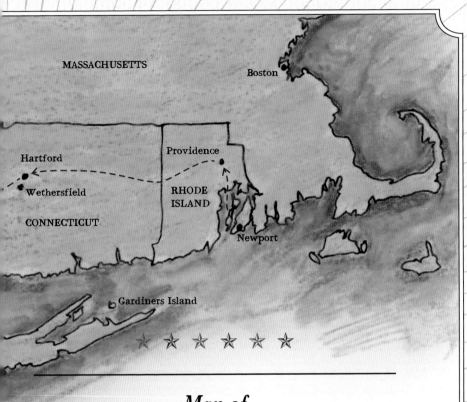

Map of
NEW ENGLAND

The French army under Rochambeau arrived on American soil in July 1780 and made Newport, Rhode Island, their base. The American army was encamped roughly 150 miles to the west in the area of White Plains, New York. Over the next year, Generals Washington and Rochambeau met three times to strategize: in Hartford and Wethersfield, Connecticut, and in Newport. At their May 1781 meeting, they decided to join forces, and in July, the French army marched west and set up camp near the Americans.

The French record of the meeting painted a most flattering portrait with various people writing a description:

"He is very tall in stature. He has a noble air, a fine face. His temperament is cool but mild and affable. His demeanor is easy and inspires confidence. He often has the impression of thought depicted on his face."

"His dignified address, his simplicity of manners, and mild gravity surpassed our expectation and won every heart."

"His face is handsome and majestic but at the same time kind and gentle, corresponding with his moral qualities."

"He looks like a hero; he is very cold and says little but he is frank and polite."

"There is a sadness in his countenance, which bore the stamp of all his virtues, inspired everyone with the devotion and respect due his character, increasing, if possible, the high opinion we already held of his exceptional merit."

Washington sized up Rochambeau, too. The French general was fifty-five years old, while Washington was forty-eight. Rochambeau was a veteran of wars all over central Europe. He walked with a limp from a war wound and exhibited a battle scar over his left temple. Compared to Washington, he was short and stocky, standing at five feet six inches tall. Rochambeau had not expected to be in America meeting General Washington, because he had been planning his military retirement. It was only days away when this new assignment came.

The fact that Rochambeau placed himself under Washington's leadership was unheard-of in French history. One of France's best generals would be fighting under a foreign commander who had not even been introduced to the king. One reason may have been the trust King Louis XVI placed in Lafayette's assessment of Washington.

A blue silk flag with thirteen six-pointed stars
representing the thirteen colonies marked General
Washington's presence wherever he went. It was
sometimes called the Commander-in-Chief's flag.

During the two-day meeting, the leaders discussed a joint attack on the British. Where? When? They agreed that they needed more manpower before they could attack, especially naval reinforcements. The two main options for a location were New York City and the South. They also briefly considered another invasion of Canada, which they had attempted in the war's first year. Washington wanted New York; Rochambeau preferred the South. Both admitted that they could not plan any attack the rest of the calendar year. Washington admitted to hoping for fifteen thousand combined troops, and Rochambeau reiterated that more were promised to him. Much to Washington's disappointment, the meeting ended with little accomplishment and no firm plan. He wrote to James Duane in Congress: "We could only combine possible plans on the supposition of possible events and engage mutually to do everything in our powers against the next campaign."

Washington and his entourage began the journey back to New York. He had no idea that his world was about to be shaken by the biggest betrayal of the war.

CHAPTER

4

A TRAITOR EXPOSED

☆ ☆ ☆ ☆ ☆ ☆ ☆ ☆ ☆ ☆ ☆ ☆ ☆ ☆ ☆ ☆ ☆ ☆

O n his return from Hartford, Washington planned to stop at West Point, an American fortress on the west bank of the Hudson River sixty miles above New York City. He had recently made one of his most trusted generals, Benedict Arnold, commander of the fort. Arnold had fought with distinction earlier in the war and became a war hero when his leg was wounded at the Battle of Saratoga. Washington then appointed him military governor of Philadelphia after

Benedict Arnold began his Revolutionary War military career as a captain in the Connecticut militia. Five years later, he had risen to major general and became the most famous traitor in American history.

the British evacuated the city. Accused of trying to profit from the war, Arnold insisted on a court-martial to clear his name. He grew increasingly bitter by what he perceived as personal injustice when Congress refused him several promotions.

Colonel Hamilton went on ahead to Arnold's headquarters south of West Point to prepare for Washington's visit. When he arrived, Arnold was nowhere to be found, and no one seemed to know where he was. A short time later, Washington's party rode up, expecting Arnold to greet them. Where was he? Even

Arnold's wife, Peggy, did not greet them. After eating a leisurely breakfast, Washington's party took Arnold's barge two miles upriver to West Point. Again, no one appeared to greet Washington. He examined the fortifications, alarmed at their poor state. Growing increasingly annoyed, he headed back to Arnold's house.

Later that day, Washington received a parcel of correspondence from his staff in which the ugly truth began to emerge. To everyone's utter shock, Arnold had defected to the British and had leaked military secrets to the enemy—he had betrayed his country. Arnold had informed the British of the general's travel plans. A plot to kidnap Washington during this trip was underway.

Fortunately, Arnold's note detailing the travel itinerary had not gotten to the British in time for them to act. But he had clearly activated a plan to allow the British to capture West Point. Washington was furious! Arnold had fled that morning and was

West Point sits at a strategic location on the Hudson River in New York and lays claim as the oldest continuously occupied military post in the United States. Today it is home to the United States Military Academy.

now safe with the British. Since the plot had been discovered in time, the fort was in no danger. Hamilton wrote to General Nathanael Greene, "There has been unfolded at this place a scene of the blackest treason."

The Americans had captured British officer John André, Arnold's contact, who was carrying letters written in Arnold's handwriting proving his treachery. In an effort to punish Arnold, Washington requested an exchange, but the British refused. André was tried as a spy, convicted, and hanged. Lafayette wrote, "I cannot describe . . . to what degree I am astounded by this piece of news . . . that Arnold, a man . . . who had given proof of talent, of Patriotism, and, especially, of the most brilliant courage, should at once destroy his very existence and should sell his country to the tyrants whom he had fought against with glory . . . [it] confounds and distresses me . . . [and] humiliates me to a degree I cannot express."

Washington rushed to reassure Rochambeau that all was well. He wrote, "By a lucky accident a conspiracy of the most dangerous kind . . . has been defeated. General Arnold, who has sullied his former glory, by the blackest treason, has escaped to the enemy." Rochambeau replied, "I know not whether I should pity you, or congratulate you upon the discovery of Arnold's frightful plot . . . it proves to us that Providence is for us and for our cause."

The British made Arnold a brigadier general in their army and gave him command of a force of more than two thousand soldiers. Washington wanted desperately to capture Arnold, put him on trial, and make him an example to the world. He initiated a secret plot that would send a sergeant major named John Champe, of Virginia, to the British lines posing as a deserter. Champe would enlist with the British in Arnold's company, then

Benedict Arnold's oath of loyalty. As an American officer, Benedict Arnold was required to denounce loyalty to King George III and sign an oath of allegiance to the United States.

organize an elaborate kidnapping that would bring Arnold back to the Americans. It was very risky, but Champe was willing. The plan was working well until the unexpected happened: In mid-December, Arnold's unit was suddenly ordered south. Before the final details of the capture plan could be put into place, Champe found himself on a ship with Arnold on the way to Virginia, to fight against his own state and his own people, who would think he was a traitor.

CHAPTER

5

PLUNDERING VIRGINIA

V irginia, the largest and wealthiest of the thirteen American colonies, stretched from the Atlantic Ocean to the Appalachian Mountains and beyond (including the present-day states of West Virginia, Kentucky, Indiana, Illinois, and portions of Ohio and western Pennsylvania). The flat, eastern part was called the Tidewater region, because the moving tides sculpted an area of rich soils perfect for growing the colony's cash crop: tobacco. Before the war about 70 percent of all the tobacco exported

At age thirty-three, Thomas Jefferson was one of the youngest delegates to the Continental Congress, where he became the primary author of the Declaration of Independence. During the war, he served one term as Virginia's governor and would later become the United States' third president.

from the colonies came from Virginia. Many farmers had become wealthy due to the great demand for the product in Europe.

The crop's cultivation was labor-intensive and required constant care. A cruel economic system relying on slave labor had taken root and flourished, based on the import of captive people from Africa. European slave traders had brought cargoes of enslaved Africans to North America starting in the early 1600s. Slavery was more widely practiced in the Southern colonies, but it was legal and existed in all thirteen.

At this time in America, the majority of people with African heritage were enslaved. Nearly 40 percent of Virginia's population was composed of enslaved Africans.

Thomas Jefferson, author of the Declaration of Independence, was currently serving in his second year as governor of the state of Virginia. On New Year's Day, 1781, he was enjoying some fresh air in the garden at his Richmond town house. A messenger on horseback rode up with a note from Brigadier General Thomas Nelson Jr., a Virginia militia commander from Yorktown. It read:

> This moment Commodore Barron [has] come in the *Liberty* out of the [Chesapeake] Bay and his report to me was that a fleet of 27 Sail [ships] is just below Willoughby point . . . This is all at present, he turned his boat about and is gone to make further discoveries.

The immediate assumption was that this mysterious armada was the British. False alarms were a regular occurrence, though, and Governor Jefferson was not about to call up the state militia for every possible threat. Thankfully, Virginia had not seen much of the British in the previous four years since Virginia militias had driven the last royal governor, John Dunmore, and his troops from the state in 1776. British troops had made occasional raids from the water, but no forces had stayed there any length of time. But, to Jefferson's great frustration, the state's military forces were not prepared to defend the state if the British did appear. The state militia was poorly organized and armed and widely dispersed, and Virginia's small navy was ineffective. And, the state legislature, now meeting in the new capital city of Richmond, had trouble passing legislation. If this was a British force, the state could be in serious trouble.

Brigadier General Benedict Arnold worried that someone might want to kill him. Once his treachery was discovered and word spread, he became the most reviled man in America. He was now in a precarious position of his own making. Though he was a high-ranking officer in the British army, the other British officers didn't trust him because he had betrayed his own military. The American rebels despised him, and Congress had put a price on his head. Anyone who captured him would receive a reward and a hero's adulation. Born and raised in the Northern colony of Connecticut, Arnold had never set foot in Virginia or the South. Virginians, generally known for their hospitality, would hardly be welcoming to the traitor.

General Sir Henry Clinton in New York, the commander of all British forces in North America, did not entirely trust Arnold's leadership skills or his motives. He thought Arnold would have been more useful to the British cause if he had remained working for the Americans and fed the British information. But Arnold had defected, and Clinton needed to find an assignment for him. He sent Arnold to Virginia with some seventeen hundred of his troops and a fleet of forty-two ships. The army included German troops that Britain had hired in Europe to supplement their army, one an elite unit called the Jägers (hunters), under the command of Captain Johann von Ewald, a rare German who respected the Americans. Ewald had joined the German military at age sixteen

Johann von Ewald, a German military officer from Hesse-Kassel, fought with the British in the American Revolution beginning in 1776. He was taken prisoner at Yorktown and eventually released on parole in a prisoner exchange. He returned to Europe in 1784.

and lost an eye in a duel. With a glass eye and a partially disfigured face, he was a soldier for hire. He kept a diary throughout the war.

Arnold's mission was to destroy arms depots; establish a base at Portsmouth, at the southern end of the Chesapeake Bay; and build a force of loyalists. Arnold would follow orders, but on his own terms. He knew this was an opportunity to demonstrate his leadership skills to his new superiors. They were watching him closely, and he wanted to prove himself. Would he show any mercy to his fellow Americans? Always trying to improve his personal financial situation, Arnold would also be looking for ways to put money into his pockets.

Arnold arrived in Virginia on the last day of 1780 and immediately took control of the waterways and started to pillage and terrorize coastal towns. He began with Newport News, where his troops destroyed property and seized boats filled with tobacco. His presence was immediately reported to Jefferson. New Year's Day was his second day in the state, and he continued his quest for riches, seizing more small boats loaded with tobacco. The Virginia militia was unprepared and disorganized but scrambled into action and began firing on Arnold's ships.

Regiment von Bose
Chef. Se. Excell. General–Lieutenant von Bose

Hessian regiments were named for their commander. This image depicts the Von Bose regiment named for Major General C. von Bose. The regiment arrived in America in August 1776 and fought with the British army.

One would think that Arnold would be hesitant to reveal his presence to Virginians, knowing he was the least popular man in America. He may have felt invincible in that moment, because he sent a note to shore threatening to burn Newport News if the militia didn't stop firing on his ships. He signed it "your humble servant, B. Arnold, B Genl." The rebel guns went silent. The following day, however, near Williamsburg, he sent a courier under a truce flag with another threatening note warning the militiamen to lay down their arms and obey their king. The militia officer this time was Thomas Nelson Jr., who asked the courier if this British commander was the traitor Arnold. When told he was, Nelson replied that he "would not and could not give up to a traitor." And if Nelson managed to capture Arnold, he "would hang him

Mary Byrd, from Philadelphia, married one of the wealthiest men in Virginia, William Byrd III, and moved with him to his large estate on the James River.

up by the heels, according to the orders of Congress." Nelson refused to stop his guns.

Arnold decided a confrontation was not worth it and continued upriver toward the state's military storage at Richmond. He stopped at Westover Plantation, a large, ornate brick mansion and estate owned by the influential and wealthy Byrd family. Owner Mary Byrd was Arnold's wife's cousin. From Philadelphia originally, Mary had married the Virginian William Byrd III. Her brother was a former mayor of Philadelphia and had served in the Continental Congress but voted against the Declaration of Independence in 1776. The Byrd family had been torn apart by the war, with sons divided in their loyalties. Mary's husband, William, had killed himself on New Year's Day 1777, depressed by the direction that Virginia was headed and fearing personal economic ruin. Prior to the war, he had served on the Governor's Council, as an adviser to the royal governor. Most people suspected that he and Mary were loyal to the Crown. Despite these suspicions, Mary's neighbors left her alone, perhaps because they pitied her unstable financial situation.

If Mary was a loyalist, it was in her best interest to keep her mouth shut. Early in the war, before the patriot cause had reached its current popularity, citizens loyal to Britain had been vocal. But as the royal governor's troops were driven away and the rebels took over Virginia's government, some loyalists had packed up and departed for Britain while they still could, leaving their homes vacant or in the care of tenants. It became increasingly dangerous for those who stayed behind to proclaim loyalty to the Crown. A loyalist might be put in prison, have his property confiscated, or be chased from his home. Since no British-held areas existed close to Virginia to offer protection, many loyalists stayed put and even signed oaths of loyalty to the state. Some fled to join the British army. Mary had once called Westover "the most delightful place in the world." She was not about to leave it.

Arnold's troops settled in at Westover, creating a base for operations around the countryside. The neighbors did wonder: Had the British been invited, or had they invited themselves? The soldiers took food, livestock, forage, two ferry boats, horses, and forty-nine slaves. Arnold assured Mary that she would be compensated for what he confiscated. Her neighbors remained suspicious of her, and she later wrote Governor Jefferson to defend her actions: "I wish well to all mankind, to America in particular. What am I but an American? All my friends and connections are in America; my whole property is here—could I wish ill to everything I have an interest in?"

Just next door to Westover sat another plantation, owned by Benjamin Harrison V, who had signed the Declaration of Independence representing Virginia. He was also Speaker of the House of Delegates, Virginia's legislature. Notified of the approaching British troops days before, Harrison had sent his family away from the area and fled to Richmond. When British troops landed on his property, slaves met them. The soldiers invited the slaves to flee to the British and gain their freedom. Arnold, the former patriot, viewed Harrison as a traitor. He directed his men to tear the Harrison family portraits off the walls and torch them in a bonfire on the front yard. The British also destroyed furniture and a large portion of the house and crops and freed forty or so slaves. The portraits and furniture next door at Westover were undisturbed.

Only thirty miles separated Westover from Richmond. A small trading post turned capital city on the James River, the town's roughly six hundred inhabitants lived in wood-frame houses spread out over two hills. No official government buildings existed yet. The governor resided in a town house, and the legislature met in a temporary building near the river. But the town did hold some tempting targets for Arnold: a foundry for producing metal, a magazine storing weapons, and warehouses, all filled with supplies for the rebel armies. Arnold decided to take a force of nine hundred men, including Captain Johann von Ewald's German regiments, to raid the town. His main interest was destroying war-related supplies and manufacturing operations, but when the opportunity to plunder presented itself, he wouldn't pass it up.

Arnold's invasion succeeded. Richmond's small militia ran, leaving no defense. The British appeared at the governor's house and inquired about Jefferson. Years later, a formerly enslaved man named Isaac recalled his conversation:

"Where is the governor?" a British officer demanded.

"He's gone to the mountains," responded a slave.

"Where are the keys of the house?"

"Mr. Jefferson left with them."

"Where is the silver?"

"It was all sent up to the mountain." The slaves had really

hidden it in various spots throughout the house, including in a bed mattress.

The soldiers proceeded to plunder the house, stealing food and drink, along with seven or so slaves. An enslaved man later recalled that "it seemed like the day of judgment was come."

Arnold's troops moved through the town, looting supplies and burning buildings. Arnold later reported their destruction: 2 warehouses, 21 carriages, 2,200 small arms, 4,000 French musket locks, and 50 bolts of canvas. They took what they wanted and torched the houses. They raided wine cellars and poured wine and whiskey into the street, so much that the roaming hogs got drunk. The soldiers robbed shops and churches and confiscated rum and grain. Ewald wrote in his diary that "terrible things happened on this excursion; churches and holy places were plundered." Soon half the town was in flames.

The troops then moved to the military targets. They attacked the foundry at Westham, where many weapons were made, and poured barrels of gunpowder into the James River. They captured foundry workers, blew up the magazine and its seven hundred barrels of powder, and destroyed machinery and two mills. The ground shook from the "many explosions [that] happened in different parts of the building . . . and the foundry was totally destroyed," wrote one British officer.

A parade of forty-two ships filled with loot, from both private citizens' homes and public buildings, stretched for miles from Richmond to Westover. In his report after the raid, Arnold claimed he had offered a deal to Jefferson to pay for half of the items stolen if the citizens would give him several hostages and offer to transport the stolen items to boats in the river. Word was taken to Jefferson, who had escaped with his family.

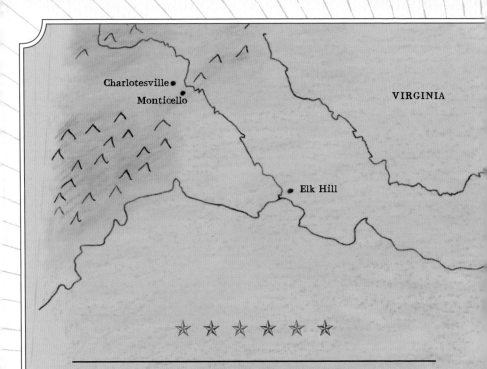

Map of

VIRGINIA

✳ ✳ ✳ ✳ ✳ ✳

The people of Virginia did not see much of the British military until Benedict Arnold and his troops showed up at the beginning of 1781 and began raiding cities and towns. Arnold used Westover as a base to attack the capital, Richmond. General Cornwallis and his troops marched up from the south and joined Arnold at Petersburg. Cornwallis's cavalry terrorized central Virginia, and his troops ventured as far west as Charlottesville, where the state legislature and the governor had fled for safety. The British then moved east, closer to the water. They initially built a base in Portsmouth, but ultimately decided on Yorktown.

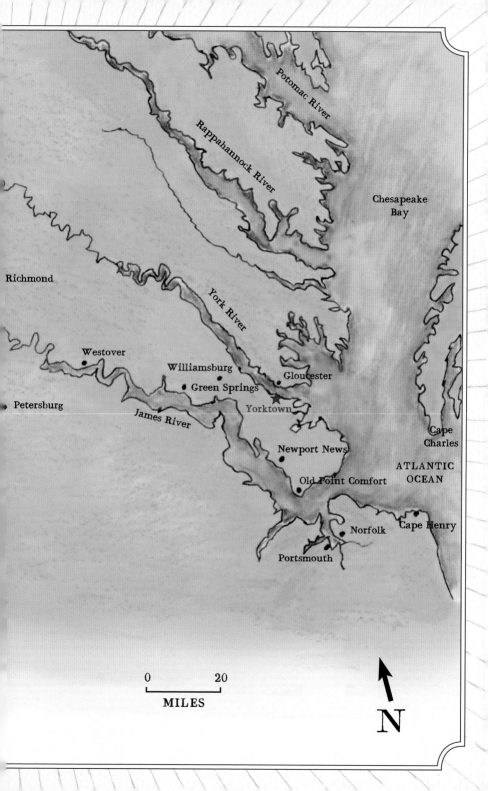

Potomac River

Rappahannock River

Chesapeake
Bay

Richmond

York River

Westover

Williamsburg

Green Springs

Gloucester

Yorktown

James River

Petersburg

Newport News

Old Point Comfort

Cape
Charles

ATLANTIC
OCEAN

Norfolk

Cape Henry

Portsmouth

0   20

MILES

N

He promptly refused any deal with the traitor. Arnold's report blamed the pillaging on Jefferson's refusal to make a deal. Assuming Jefferson was in hiding nearby, Arnold wrote later, "As Mr. Jefferson was so inattentive to the preservation of private property, I found myself under the disagreeable necessity of a large quantity of rum to be [stored], several warehouses of salt to be destroyed; several public storehouses and smith's shops with their contents were consumed by flames." Arnold also tried to place responsibility on his men, claiming that "private property was burnt without my order by an officer who was informed it was public property."

Jefferson didn't know what Arnold's mission was; he only realized he faced a force that could move at will around his state, destroying both government and private property. And Arnold could be staying for a while. Jefferson began sending pleas to General Washington in New York, begging for help from his army. Could he spare troops for his home state? Could Washington himself come? Virginia militias would most certainly rally around the leader of the American army.

Washington read the requests. The traitor Benedict Arnold was terrorizing his home state. The general couldn't tolerate this. Reports from Virginia called Arnold's troops "infamous beasts," and Baron von Closen, an aide and interpreter for General Rochambeau with the French troops in Newport, wrote in his diary, "All the letters from Virginia are full of lamentations over the horrors and [plundering] that Arnold's detachment is committing there."

Washington decided to send Lafayette's light infantry to Virginia to meet up with a militia unit commanded by Baron von Steuben, a German who was the highest-ranking officer of the Continental Army in Virginia. The goal was to capture Arnold and hang him. Washington's orders to Lafayette stated: "You are to do no act whatever with Arnold that directly or by implication may screen him from the punishment due to his treason and desertion, which if he should fall into your hands, you will execute in the most [prompt] way."

As a sign of his esteem, Washington gave Lafayette command of a light infantry detachment of twelve hundred, composed of select soldiers from New York, Connecticut, Massachusetts, Pennsylvania, and New Hampshire units. Their distinctive French-made uniforms included red and black plumes on each helmet. They trained and drilled hard and soon became known throughout the American army for their closeness and professionalism. Light infantries were trained and equipped for quick movement, skirmishes (clashes with small groups of soldiers), and reconnaissance (observation of the enemy). The horse division carried its own flags that Lafayette had brought from France. They read in Latin, *Ultimo Ratio* (Ultimate Reckoning), meant to inspire fear in the enemy. Lafayette wrote, "I had returned from France with a costly collection of ornaments for my soldiers, swords for officers and their junior officers, and banners for the battalions. This troop of chosen men, well drilled and disciplined, were easily recognized by their [uniforms]." Astride his white horse, which he had bought for himself, Lafayette was more than ready to go into battle, the very image of a French knight.

Lafayette and his unit departed their New York encampment on February 22, headed south on what would be his most important assignment thus far. If successful, it would end with Arnold on the gallows.

Meanwhile, Governor Jefferson came up with an enticing plan of his own to deal with Arnold. Jefferson had lost confidence in local militias. He authorized his military leaders to recruit men from the frontier with excellent marksmanship skills. Jefferson gave his leadership permission to "reveal to [the frontiersmen] our desire, and engage them [to] undertake to seize and bring off this greatest of traitors." If they were successful in capturing Arnold alive, they would receive a handsome cash reward and "their names will be recorded with glory in history."

The longer Arnold stayed in Virginia, the more nervous he became about being captured alive. He surrounded himself with guards and always carried two small pistols in his pockets for added protection. He had struck up a conversation with a captured American captain. "What should be my fate if I should be taken prisoner?" he had asked the man. The prisoner responded, "They will cut off that shortened leg of yours wounded at Quebec and Saratoga, and bury it with all the honors of war, and then hang the rest of you on a gibbet [scaffold]."

Arnold moved back to Portsmouth, where he had first arrived, back to his original mission to build defenses to guard the entrance of the Chesapeake Bay that led to the Atlantic Ocean. The shallow bay cut through the colony and served as a major water highway north and south for the Middle Atlantic colonies. The narrow entrance of the bay was a crucial crossroads, because control of this area meant control of any traffic entering from the ocean.

The Virginia militias gathered close by, growing in numbers. Virginia's military leaders began developing a plan to attack Arnold. Word that a French fleet sailing south from Rhode Island would soon arrive only added to the anticipation. If Lafayette and his troops could meet up with the militias and a French fleet could block any Royal Navy support, they might be able to dislodge Arnold and his British troops from the state.

CHAPTER

6

HAPPY BIRTHDAY, GENERAL

The French forces of nearly six thousand men were spending the winter of 1781 in Newport, Rhode Island, an old New England city hugging the coast of the Atlantic Ocean roughly 220 miles away from Washington's army in New York. Newport had been a hotbed for the patriots until the British army occupied it for three years beginning in 1776. Half the city's population of nine thousand fled. The arrival of the French made the people of Newport nervous, having just endured an enemy occupation. For some residents, the troops felt like another European invasion. With the French language heard on all the street corners, it almost seemed like one. Rochambeau met with the citizens and explained that the French were there at Washington's request, and he assured them his soldiers would be disciplined and pay for what they needed in silver coin. This promise of hard money got their attention. The French were welcome!

The soldiers represented a mixture of French society: small farmers and laborers, artisans, minor nobility. Most were single men between eighteen and thirty, the youngest a fourteen-year-old drummer boy, the oldest, sixty-one. While the officers had volunteered to fight for America, most of the soldiers had not even known when they embarked that America was their destination. The French impressed the Newport citizens. One merchant commented that the French officers "are the most civilized men I ever met. They are temperate, prudent, and extremely attentive to duty."

A South West

View of Newport.

Newport, Rhode Island, a major trade center, was also known for religious freedom. Baptists found a home there, as did Jews and Quakers. The nation's oldest synagogue, Touro, stands in Newport.

☆ ☆ ☆

Because of the cold weather, winter was a down time for both armies. But spring was around the corner, yet Rochambeau had no clear plan moving forward to fulfill his mission: France had come to help Washington win the war. He was feeling a bit neglected by General Washington. After the two generals' first and only meeting in Hartford the previous fall, Washington had faced the betrayal of Benedict Arnold and understandably had to give that mess his attention.

On February 23, Rochambeau decided to send Washington a note: "Yesterday was Your Excellency's birthday. We have put off celebrating that holiday until today by reason of the Lord's day, and we will celebrate it with the sole regret that Your Excellency is not a witness to the gladness of our hearts." The note got Washington's attention—he was touched by its sentiment and said he would visit Newport very soon.

Immediately, Rochambeau sent his aide Baron von Closen, a blond, blue-eyed German, to escort Washington to Newport. The general and his Life Guards rode through Connecticut and arrived at Newport on March 6. Closen wrote in his diary, "The arrival of General Washington . . . created a general sensation throughout the army and among all the residents of Newport and the surrounding area. All the fleet was decked with flags and saluted him with 13 cannon shots."

A barge transported Washington, Closen, and others out to the *Duc de Bourgogne*, anchored in Newport's harbor, where all the French naval officers and Rochambeau greeted them. After a short sail, they arrived at Long Wharf to another welcoming gun salute. They marched to Rochambeau's headquarters with "all the pomp and ceremony accorded to a marshal of France [a

No 1.

GAZETTE FRANÇOISE.

Du Vendredi 17 Novembre 1780.

Le projet de donner une Gazette Françaiſe, ne m'a paru poſſible que par la facilité d'y introduire la Traduction des différentes Nouvelles que les Papiers Américains produiſent : c'eſt ſous ce point de vue que j'en ai accepté la rédaction ; vraiſemblablement ceux de MM. les Officiers & autres Particuliers qui ne ſont pas familiers avec la langue du pays, & qui s'intéreſſent aux évennemens politiques de cette Nation naiſſante, ſeront charmés de pouvoir s'en inſtruire, ſans avoir recours au travail de la tranſlation. Je ne m'engagerai donc envers le Public, qu'à répéter en Français, ce que les Américains auront dit dans leur langue. D'ailleurs, peu accoutumé à me faire imprimer, j'ai beſoin dans cette entrepriſe, de toute l'indulgence de mes Lecteurs. Je vous ſupplie donc Meſſieurs, ſi cet Ouvrage peut toucher votre curioſité, de le protéger de vos bontés. Je me ferai un devoir de recevoir les avis de ceux qui me feront l'honneur de s'y intéreſſer, & d'agir conformément à leurs conſeils.

La Gazette Françoise was published by the French navy in Newport from 1780 to 1781 and was the first French newspaper printed in what would become the United States.

To help ease the long winter, the French often held weekly balls, which brought locals and their visitors together and helped the officers learn English and the locals, French. Few Newport residents spoke the language. The army even started a short-term French-language newspaper, the *Gazette Françoise*. Printed on a press that had crossed the Atlantic, it aimed to keep primarily French officers unable to read English informed of current events—current in this case meaning the past six to eight months. Higher-ranking officers lodged with Newport families and frequently gave—and received—private language lessons from the daughters of their hosts.

top honor] or a prince." Newport's town council, excited about Washington's visit, distributed free candles to residents to put in their windows and illuminate the town. That evening, the whole town glowed in light for a procession of Washington, his staff, and the French officers through the streets. Thirty boys carrying lighted candles on long sticks led the procession. Later that evening, city officials hosted an elegant ball in Washington's honor.

Despite the merriment, Washington was not pleased. His intelligence sources had recently informed him that the Royal Navy was planning to send ships from their Long Island base to the Chesapeake Bay very soon. Britain knew of the presence of the French navy and was not about to give France control of the bay. There was no time to lose. When Washington arrived in Newport, he was hoping to see the French fleet ready to leave; instead, he saw it decked out with flags to welcome him. Action. He wanted action!

The next two days were filled with dinners, suppers, and balls meant to show both the city's and the French army's high regard for Washington. Despite all the diplomatic courtesies, underneath the celebrations were ulterior motives. To Washington, his meetings with Rochambeau were all about establishing trust. For Washington to work closely with the French, he had to trust them. And that meant believing that their motives for wanting to help were good. He had had early misgivings about a foreign country sending troops onto American soil to help the patriot cause. Washington had his own personal history with French soldiers: He had been their prisoner as a young man, during the French and Indian War. That war had been a grab for territory. What was France's intent now?

Washington was looking for the French to take some action

and to show they were willing to work with him. The French admiral planned to send a fleet of eight ships of the line and several frigates south with twelve hundred troops to bolster Lafayette's army (which had not made it to Virginia yet). Their combined goal was to capture Benedict Arnold and stop his activities in Virginia. Washington hoped these ships would transport Lafayette's men down the Chesapeake Bay to the British troops, but the French commanders said this was not possible. Washington suspected it had to do with the general refusal of French officers to serve under the young Lafayette. They thought he did not have enough experience, but only had Washington's favor. Washington was annoyed by the seeming desire of the French to make their own plans without consulting him. This was not teamwork.

Finally, at midday on March 8, as Washington and Rochambeau watched from a hill overlooking the harbor, the fleet set sail. It promptly ran aground on the point, in full view of the commanders. After a few hours more to fix the problem, the fleet continued on its way. Could the French beat the British ships to the Chesapeake?

Thirty-six hours later, a British fleet of eight ships of the line and accompanying support ships left Gardiners Island, fifty miles southwest of Newport, headed south. The race was on. Admiral Marriot Arbuthnot knew his British ships had one big advantage: The entire fleet had been sheathed in copper plates, a new technological improvement that gave them a speed advantage. Only a few French ships had this feature. Could they catch the French?

Eight days after leaving Newport, early in the morning on March 16, the French fleet was just east of Cape Henry, at the entrance of the Chesapeake Bay. The sea was rough, and a storm was brewing. The lookout suddenly signaled "Sail ahead!" The

Le Vaisseau du Roi portant le pavillon de M. le Comte au combat de Chesapeack.

British fleet materialized out of the fog, blocking the French from their destination. The British had won the race. The French plan had been to sail without obstacle into the bay, unload the soldiers, capture Arnold, and return north, not engage in a full-scale naval battle with the British. Charles Destouches, the temporary acting

"Le Conquérant" de La Grandière. Chef d'Escadre, le 16 Mars, 1781.

This engraving shows the French ship of the line *Le Conquerant*, center, taking heavy fire from British ships on March 16, 1781, during the First Battle of the Capes.

French commander, was unexpectedly forced to decide whether he wanted to engage the Royal Navy. Even if he managed to get past the British, they would most likely follow him and fire on his ships while they attempted to disembark the soldiers.

However, it turned out not to be Destouches's decision. Since the winds were in his favor, Admiral Arbuthnot decided to force a battle, despite poor visibility due to rain. At his command, the cannons began to roar, and the massive ships aimed their best shots at the French. For more than an hour, the British maintained the advantage. Cannonballs ripped into heavy wooden beams, splinters flying. But Destouches did not give up, and the advantage soon changed. The gun decks shook as the rigging and masts and sails on the British ships were destroyed. After two hours of fighting in the driving rain, Admiral Arbuthnot was finished. His flagship, HMS *London*, the largest ship in either fleet, had lost its main topsail yard. The French had suffered more casualties, but their ships had received less damage. A British officer later wrote: "If Admiral Arbuthnot tells the truth, he must confess to the eternal disgrace of our navy, that with a much superior fleet both in number and size of ships, he behaved as shamefully ill as the French behaved gallantly well." The French had outgunned the mighty British navy and were now in a strong position to sail into the Chesapeake and capture Arnold. But, to Arbuthnot's surprise, they didn't. They turned around and sailed back to Newport!

Lafayette couldn't believe it either. He had sailed down the Chesapeake in a small boat because his army was stuck at the top of the bay with no transportation. He had witnessed the militia forces closing in on Arnold at Portsmouth and was feeling positive that something would go his way in Virginia. He later wrote Governor Jefferson describing his disappointment and saying, "This however may be a satisfaction that on our part we have been perfectly ready, and that with a naval superiority our success would have been certain." Victory had been so close, yet Arnold remained free to continue his pillage of Virginia.

Destouches later said he had retreated because he had not

been aware of the extent of the damage his fleet had inflicted on the British. He had assessed his losses and felt it unwise to continue the fight. His temporary status of commander may have also impacted his decision and made him more cautious.

☆ ☆ ☆

General Washington did not receive news of what would later be called the First Battle of the Capes until two weeks later. Once again, frustration welled inside him. He conveyed his feelings in a letter to his cousin in Virginia. They could have destroyed Arnold! How could the French turn back? Again, he mentioned the delays in Newport.

The commander in chief knew better than to trust the mail. He constantly advised his officers to avoid writing something they didn't want intercepted. Unfortunately, the British seized a sack of mail containing the letter to his cousin, and it ended up in one of New York's loyalist newspapers. The French were not amused. He responded to Rochambeau that the letter's publication had caused him "extreme pain," but he never felt the need to apologize. While it most likely embarrassed him, the letter ultimately may have helped him by clearly communicating his feelings to the French.

Washington wrote in his journal on May 1, 1781: "Instead of having anything in readiness to take the field, we have nothing; and instead of having the prospect of having a glorious offensive campaign before, we have a bewildered and gloomy prospect of a defensive one; unless we should receive a powerful aid of ships, troops, and money from our generous allies [France]."

Seven months earlier, Rochambeau had sent his son Donatien, vicomte de Rochambeau, to the French king to ask for more help. They needed additional troops if they wanted to dislodge the British from New York City. After what seemed a very long wait, Donatien's ship finally returned in early May at Boston. Aboard was the new admiral for the fleet at Newport, the comte de Barras, replacing Destouches. The younger Rochambeau brought bad and good news. The bad news was that the king had rejected the request for more ground troops. The good news was that he had approved more aid from the French navy. Another large fleet, under Admiral de Grasse, was on its way from France, headed to a base in the West Indies, close to America, and would be available for action in North America. Along with news, Donatien Rochambeau also brought a lot of money to help the American cause.

Still, Rochambeau was disappointed. He really needed more soldiers if an attack on New York was to work. In any case, a plan for the summer months was crucial. It was time once again to meet with Washington. It was also time to connect the American and French troops. If they were going to fight together, they should be living closer to each other.

A third meeting of the two leaders took place later that month, on May 21, in Wethersfield, Connecticut. At the meeting, they still did not agree on a strategy moving forward, though Rochambeau did consent to move his troops to White Plains, New York, nearer the Continental troops. Washington still believed a full-scale attack on the British army occupying New York City should be the goal. Rochambeau still thought a Virginia location for an attack would be better. Washington's argument was that a Virginia campaign would require a major transportation of troops; it was a long, hot march, they would probably lose men to illness, and it would require naval control of the Chesapeake Bay, which they didn't have. An attack on New York City, on the other hand, would force the British to withdraw troops from Virginia and send them north, relieving stress on Virginia. Rochambeau's argument was that New York was well fortified with seasoned troops, thus hard to capture. Also, the large French ships required deeper water than the British ships, and a sandbar at Sandy Hook, near New York City, posed a challenge. The French ships would not risk going over it.

Rochambeau ultimately agreed to support Washington's final decision, but he arranged to stay flexible until an obvious course of action became clearer. In any case, Rochambeau assured Washington that Admiral de Grasse's larger French fleet would be in American waters at the end of the summer. Between French naval ships already in the Caribbean, the planned addition of de Grasse's fleet there, and the ships in Newport, he was confident the French could attain naval superiority. And so, the French began to make plans to move the army from Newport to New York. This would improve communication and help the allies learn to trust each other. Privately, though, Rochambeau had grave doubts about the American army's ability to finish the war it had started. He wrote Admiral de Grasse that "the Americans are at the end of their resources, that Washington will not have half of the troops he is reckoned to have." He suggested that de Grasse bring as many soldiers as he could.

CHAPTER

7

THE PERFECT SPY

☆ ☆ ☆ ☆ ☆ ☆ ☆ ☆ ☆ ☆ ☆ ☆ ☆ ☆ ☆ ☆

Military plans often run into unexpected obstacles. Lafayette's troops got held up in Maryland, waiting on transportation. Lafayette had traveled to Virginia without them, to do some reconnaissance and to meet with the state's military leaders. Then, the disappointing naval battle occurred. Ten days after the battle, a new British fleet arrived in the Chesapeake Bay with twenty-two hundred soldiers and Major General

Thomas Jefferson supposedly described British General William Phillips, portrayed here, as "the proudest man of the proudest nation on Earth."

eral William Phillips. Earlier in the war, Phillips, a well-respected officer, had surrendered with the British at the Battle of Saratoga to an American force including Arnold. Now he would be Arnold's commanding officer. Coincidentally, while a prisoner of war near Charlottesville, he had visited Thomas Jefferson at his home, Monticello, only two years previously. He had been freed in a prisoner exchange and was now back in the war. Arnold and Phillips's combined force numbered forty-five hundred soldiers. It was late March 1781, and Jefferson now had even more British troops in his state.

Frustrated, Lafayette realized that at present, an attack had no hope of succeeding, given the numbers. He returned to his troops in Maryland. They would march into Virginia, since no water transport was available, and he would decide a new plan of action once there.

To capture Benedict Arnold, Lafayette needed more information: eyes and ears inside the British camps. How could he stay one step ahead of the British and anticipate their next action? He would recruit spies. One thing he had learned from General Washington was the importance of developing an intelligence network of spies. As a young man fighting with the British against the French on the frontier, Washington had discovered the value of espionage and deception. Both sides used spies to gather crucial information about the activities of the enemy. Early in the Revolution, Washington had written, "There is one evil I dread, and that is, [British] spies." He knew what he was up against. Washington had started from nothing and built his own intelligence operation. In the past several years, he had guided the development of an effective spy ring around New York that brought him valuable information.

Good spies knew how to stay out of sight, to conceal their identity in order to avoid notice, to travel incognito and blend in. They were loyal and stealthy. Lafayette began looking for someone who would not raise any suspicion, who would draw no attention to himself. He needed someone to go among the British officers and learn as much as possible, then communicate this intelligence back to him. Who could gain access to the British? It hit him: an enslaved person! Slaves were used to doing their work and blending into the background. He knew the British officers used slaves as servants. Perhaps his spy could even get a job working for a high-ranking officer. He would be able to overhear conversations and to read documents lying around.

☆ ☆ ☆

James, an enslaved man from New Kent County, wasn't sure he had heard correctly. Standing before him was a tall, thin, boyish man, the famous French major general the Marquis de Lafayette. He looked splendid in a clean blue, white, and gold uniform, his reddish-blond hair visible under his black tricorn hat. Listening hard through the general's thick accent, James thought Lafayette was asking him to become a spy and go behind enemy lines to a British officer's camp. The British would never suspect an enslaved man would be gathering intelligence for the patriot cause. Most slaves did not know how to read. But James did. Lafayette said James would report directly to him.

What questions ran through James's mind? More than anything, he likely wanted answers to two: What would happen to him if he got caught? And could he earn his freedom if he was successful?

Everyone knew the answer to the first: death. The British were known to execute spies. They had hanged several American spies in the North earlier in the war.

Second question . . . a very complicated one. Certainly, Lafayette had no power to give James his freedom. He wasn't even American. James would need approval from his owner, William Armistead, even to participate in such a scheme. Even if James was successful as a spy and Armistead wanted to free him, Virginia law allowed owners to free a slave only for very specific reasons, and it required permission of the governor. But in this unsettled time, everything depended on the outcome of the war. There was no guarantee he would receive his freedom.

The worlds that James and Lafayette inhabited could not have been more different. James had been born into slavery on

James sat to have this portrait painted later in his life when he was about seventy-six years old and was living a quiet life in New Kent County, Virginia.

Armistead's plantation in New Kent County, in the Tidewater region of Virginia.

James didn't know the exact year he was born, around 1748. That made him about thirty-three years old. He had grown up in the Virginia countryside, surrounded by an enslaved community that surely dreamed about what life would be like as free people. The Armisteads were merchants who bought and sold goods. James's owner, William, had been hired as Virginia's commissary of stores (he bought and tracked all the provisions for the state's militia) and had recently coordinated the move of the public store from Williamsburg upriver to Richmond, the new capital. James was his personal servant and was familiar with many aspects of the business.

As an enslaved person, James had no power. He could not control how he managed his time, what work he did, or where he traveled. Under the law, he could be sold at any time and sent anywhere. Families were routinely torn apart when they were sold to different owners. Born enslaved due to his mother's status as a slave, based on the color of her skin, James was destined to remain a slave his entire life . . . unless he could find a way to freedom.

War often brings unexpected opportunity. Enslaved people were rarely given a choice like this. What kind of person was the Marquis de Lafayette? Could James trust him with his life? Even if James agreed to spy for Lafayette, he was still Armistead's property.

The thrill of adventure aside, was James willing to risk his life for a cause that may or may not affect his everyday life? Independence from Great Britain was a dream of the white leaders. All around him was talk of equality, justice, and rights. What did freedom ultimately mean? If, as the Declaration of Independence stated, *all* men were created equal, what did this mean for black men and women who were not considered equal?

There was no talk of freeing the thousands of enslaved Africans who toiled on the Virginia plantations.

Another option was to run to the British, who were promising freedom to slaves. Many of the escaped slaves following the British army served the officers or worked as wagoners, cooks, laundresses, and local guides. Captain Johann von Ewald, the German military officer who commanded German troops attached to the British army, wrote about them in his diary. But going to the British also required trust that they would fulfill their promise.

Could becoming a spy for the Americans somehow improve his future? Was it a gamble James was willing to take?

Yes!

Historical evidence does not reveal when and where Lafayette and James first met. The most likely places are Richmond or New Kent Courthouse, the county seat of New Kent County, where James lived. Lafayette passed through there on a number of occasions. No doubt Lafayette's and William Armistead's paths crossed numerous times due to the nature of Armistead's job. James spent a good deal of time helping Armistead. One can easily imagine Lafayette meeting James in the store.

Having grown up in the region between Williamsburg and Richmond, James knew the countryside, the roads, the creeks, the rivers. He traveled a lot because his owner's job required it. Armistead was the person in charge of supplying the officers and soldiers of Virginia's regular regiments and militias with goods and equipment. As commissary, he knew where to acquire everything from tents to drums to compasses and rope. He needed to ensure that the military was clothed as well— shirts, leggings, coats, breeches, hats, and shoes. Earlier in the war, Armistead had served as assistant commissary. His father's influence helped him get the job, but he brought experience working in an uncle's store, too. It was a big role, trying to control distribution of goods across the state.

General Phillips's orders were to help Arnold harass rebel positions, impede American supply chains, and establish a defensible post on the Chesapeake from which ships of the line could anchor and operate. As ranking general, Phillips had decided on a return trip to Richmond. When Lafayette and his troops finally reached northern Virginia on April 21, he learned that the British were headed to the capital city again, and he was determined to try to stop them. He ordered a quick hundred-mile march from Alexandria south to Richmond. They arrived just in time to confront the British forces outside the city. The Americans and the British set up on opposite banks of the wide James River, looking at each other.

Arnold and Phillips stood on the riverbank, both tempting targets. Five Virginia militiamen in hunting shirts and moccasins approached Lafayette and asked for permission to assassinate them. They were certain they could complete the job. If successful, the killings could change the entire course of the war. And Lafayette had a personal interest in the request: As an officer in the British army twenty-two years earlier, Phillips had directed the battle that had killed Lafayette's father. Lafayette did not authorize assassination, however, deciding instead

The Marquis de Lafayette, painted a few years before Yorktown. General Washington and Lafayette hired famous artist Charles Willson Peale to paint their images to exchange as a token of their mutual admiration for each other.

to stick to standard military procedure that prohibited assassinating officers.

Lafayette cleverly spread his men out to make the force look bigger than it was. The following morning, Phillips looked out at the Americans and saw a much larger army than he had expected. As a result, unsure of the exact size of the opposing force, he decided not to risk an attack. He set fire to a few tobacco warehouses and turned south to Petersburg. But Arnold's time in Virginia was up. He received orders to return to British headquarters in New York, ruining any opportunity of capture by the Americans.

Several days later, General Phillips became ill. Within a few days, he was weak, his health quickly deteriorating. While lying in bed on his ship, Phillips received a letter from Lord Cornwallis, second-in-command in North America. Big news: Cornwallis was just to the south in North Carolina, heading to Petersburg,

Virginia, near Richmond, with reinforcements. Their combined army of seven thousand soldiers would be a major force in Virginia. Both Jefferson and Major General Lafayette would have new worries.

Lafayette was still outnumbered by the British, but if General Anthony Wayne's regiment of Pennsylvanians arrived as expected, the numbers might even out. Lafayette was beginning to feel confident. He might be able to help Virginia after all.

CHAPTER

REDCOATS EQUAL FREEDOM

☆ ☆ ☆ ☆ ☆ ☆ ☆ ☆ ☆ ☆ ☆ ☆ ☆ ☆ ☆ ☆ ☆ ☆ ☆

George Washington had taken a great risk to lead the Continental Army. When he left his beloved Virginia home, Mount Vernon, at the start of the conflict, he did not know whether or not the house would still be standing when he returned. It was a potential target should the British army be nearby. In April 1781, two letters arrived for him at headquarters in New Windsor, New York. They were from his distant cousin Lund Washington, whom he had hired to manage his estate while he was away. One letter stated that a British warship had sailed up the Potomac River and stopped at Washington's home. Lund wrote that the ship had first landed men on the opposite shore in Maryland, where they had burned a number of "gentlemen's houses . . . in sight of Mount Vernon." Captain Thomas Graves of the *Savage* sent a message to the residents of Mount Vernon that he would torch the house unless he and his crew were given "a large supply of provisions." Before he left, Washington had given Lund specific instructions that he should never comply with any British demands in order to save property. In other words, Washington wanted no special treatment.

Lund refused Graves's demand. The angry captain sent a second note inviting Lund to come aboard the ship. Lund decided he should accept and boarded the ship, with a small "present of poultry." Graves "expressed his personal respect for the character of the General [Washington]," and must have charmed Lund, because after the conversation, Lund "instantly [sent] sheep,

George Washington's home, Mount Vernon, sits high on a bluff overlooking the Potomac River. Washington was away for almost the entire eight years of the war, leaving his wife, Martha, and a distant cousin to manage it.

hogs, and an abundant supply of other articles as a present to the English frigate."

In the second letter to Washington, Lund listed seventeen Mount Vernon slaves who had seized the opportunity to escape and made their way to the ship, seeking protection and freedom with the British. The fourteen men and three women included Gunner, a forty-five-year-old brickmaker; Thomas, a seventeen-year-old house servant; Stephen, a twenty-year-old cooper; and teenagers Esther and Deborah.

Then Washington received another letter about the encounter, from Lafayette, who was in Alexandria, Virginia, near Mount Vernon, at the time. He wrote:

> When the enemy came to your house many Negroes deserted to them. This piece of news did not affect me much as I little value property. But you cannot conceive how unhappy I have been to hear that Mr. Lund Washington went on board the enemy's vessel and consented to give them provisions.

He went on to admonish Washington, saying that Lund was his representative at his house and the incident would look very bad, especially to neighbors whose homes were burned. He ended by saying, "You will do what you think proper about it, my dear General, but, as your friend, it was my duty confidentially to mention the circumstances."

Washington was very angry and embarrassed and wrote to Lund on April 30: "It would have been a less painful circumstance to me, to have heard, that in consequence of your non-compliance with their request, [the British] had burnt my house and laid the plantation in ruins." It set a very bad example and was "exceedingly ill-judged."

For an enslaved person, like those at Mount Vernon, the quest for freedom was complicated: Stay in a horrible situation or escape to an unknown full of potential danger. No one could look into the future and see the outcome of the war and how black lives would be impacted by British victory or defeat. If the British succeeded in quelling the rebellion, would things return to the same as before the war? The institution of slavery in the American colonies came from the British Empire. There was no reason to assume it would be abolished. If the rebels won, would they abolish slavery? Since slave labor was a backbone of the economy, with the entire Southern region of the colonies built on it, why would this change? Or would the talk of independence and freedom lead to an abolition movement?

The Reverend Henry Muhlenburg, a Lutheran minister near Philadelphia, wrote in his diary that blacks "secretly wished that the British army might win, for then all Negro slaves will gain their freedom." He added, "It is said that this sentiment is almost universal among the Negroes in America." In 1775, Virginia's royal governor, John Dunmore, had written a proclamation urging enslaved people to run away to the British. Since then, the Union Jack flag and red-coated British soldiers had become a beacon for many slaves willing to take the risk. To them, the red coat equaled liberty.

The British military leaders faced a challenge when it came to enslaved blacks. According to laws at the time, slaves were

GREAT BRITAIN.
Union Jack.

20

The first flag of Great Britain, commonly called the
King's Colors or the Union Jack, was adopted in 1707
and combines the flags of England and Scotland.

considered "property." Clinton and Cornwallis made decisions
for military reasons, not for humane reasons: to quash the rebellion, not to help people. What policies would lead to victory
in the war? If they encouraged enslaved people to escape and
come to the British for protection, the army would need to feed,
clothe, and shelter them. The loss of escaped slaves, however,
would hurt the rebel economy. Yet the British couldn't afford to
offend the loyalist slave owners.

As the British army and navy moved through the South,
thousands of slaves risked all and flocked to them for freedom.

By His Excellency the Right Honorable JOHN Earl of DUNMORE, His Majesty's Lieutenant and Governor General of the Colony and Dominion of Virginia, and Vice Admiral of the same.

A PROCLAMATION.

AS I have ever entertained Hopes, that an Accommodation might have taken Place between GREAT-BRITAIN and this Colony, without being compelled by my Duty to this most disagreeable but now absolutely necessary Step, rendered so by a Body of armed Men unlawfully assembled, firing on His Majesty's Tenders, and the formation of an Army, and that Army now on their March to attack His Majesty's Troops and destroy the well disposed Subjects of this Colony. To defeat such treasonable Purposes, and that all such Traitors, and their Abettors, may be brought to Justice, and that the Peace, and good Order of this Colony may be again restored, which the ordinary Course of the Civil Law is unable to effect; I have thought fit to issue this my Proclamation, hereby declaring, that until the aforesaid good Purposes can be obtained, I do in Virtue of the Power and Authority to ME given, by His Majesty, determine to execute Martial Law, and cause the same to be executed throughout this Colony: and to the end that Peace and good Order may the sooner be restored, I do require every Person capable of bearing Arms, to resort to His Majesty's STANDARD, or be looked upon as Traitors to His Majesty's Crown and Government, and thereby become liable to the Penalty the Law inflicts upon such Offences; such as forfeiture of Life, confiscation of Lands, &c. &c. And I do hereby further declare all indented Servants, Negroes, or others, (appertaining to Rebels,) free that are able and willing to bear Arms, they joining His Majesty's Troops as soon as may be, for the more speedily reducing this Colony to a proper Sense of their Duty, to His Majesty's Crown and Dignity. I do further order, and require, all His Majesty's Leige Subjects, to retain their Quitrents, or any other Taxes due or that may become due, in their own Custody, till such Time as Peace may be again restored to this at present most unhappy Country, or demanded of them for their former salutary Purposes, by Officers properly authorised to receive the same.

GIVEN under my Hand on board the Ship WILLIAM, off NORFOLK, the 7th Day of NOVEMBER, in the SIXTEENTH Year of His Majesty's Reign.

DUNMORE.

(GOD save the KING.)

Virginia's Royal Governor John Dunmore intended for his November 1775 proclamation to encourage enslaved people to leave their owners. He thought this would damage the colonial economy. Note that in colonial printing an "f" is usually pronounced like an "s."

Cornwallis wondered how to respond. In South Carolina, Colonel Banastre Tarleton reported that "all the negroes, men, women, and children, upon the approach of any detachment of the King's troops, thought themselves absolved from all respect to their American masters, and entirely released from servitude. Influenced by this idea, they quitted the plantations, and followed the army." Upon leaving Charles Town, Clinton had instructed Cornwallis that "as to the Negroes, I will leave such orders as I hope will prevent the confusion that would arise from a further desertion of them to us, and I will consider some scheme of placing those we have on abandoned plantations on which they may subsist. In the meantime, Your Lordship can make such arrangements as will discourage their joining us."

A British base, such as Portsmouth or Charles Town, provided a degree of stability. The British military put black refugees to work. They didn't pay the workers, but they provided rations. More than five hundred black workers helped construct fortifications at Portsmouth. But following an army on the move was hard. Cornwallis permitted officers to have black servants. According to Johann von Ewald, every officer traveled with three or four black servants to carry baggage and do chores, as well as a black cook and maid. They also served as spies and guides for the British, since they knew the land—and where treasures might have been stored.

Cornwallis discouraged slave rebellion and issued ongoing regulations to direct the activities of these former slaves and the number of slaves that officers could utilize. Certain blacks were authorized to accompany the army's units. Cornwallis decreed in May 1781 "The number or names of Corps to be marked in a conspicuous manner on the jacket of each negro." All blacks

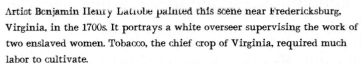

Artist Benjamin Henry Latrobe painted this scene near Fredericksburg, Virginia, in the 1700s. It portrays a white overseer supervising the work of two enslaved women. Tobacco, the chief crop of Virginia, required much labor to cultivate.

not distinguished were to be sent away from the army. Cornwallis regularly reminded commanders to allow only those blacks who were filling a need for the army to remain.

As the army moved throughout Virginia, the number of black refugees swelled. "Any place this horde approached was eaten clean . . . Where all these people lived was a riddle to me. Fortunately, the army seldom stayed in one place longer than a day or a night," recorded Captain Ewald, adding, "[Slaves] were given their freedom by the army because it was actually thought this would punish the rich, rebellious-minded inhabitants of . . . Virginia."

Virginians were taking notice and were feeling the losses. One Virginia observer, Dr. Robert Honyman, wrote that "the infatuation of these [slaves] was amazing: they flocked to the enemy from all quarters, even from very remote parts . . . some plantations were entirely cleared and not a single Negro remained." Although Cornwallis always denied that he had ordered his troops to encourage the slaves to flee, Honyman claimed that the British troops "enticed and flattered the Negroes, and [persuaded] vast numbers to go along with them, but they did not compel any." One Virginia politician wrote that some Virginians "had lost every slave they had in the world . . . force, fraud, intrigue, [and] theft" were used by British "to delude these unhappy people and defraud their masters."

Plantation owners sometimes tried to track down their slaves. In July 1781, Thomas Nelson, recently elected governor of Virginia, wrote Cornwallis about receiving frequent applications from Virginia citizens for permission to recover their slaves from the British. Nelson requested information about possible compensation. Cornwallis replied, "No Negroes have been taken by the British troops by my orders nor to my knowledge, but great numbers have come to us from different parts of the country." And then he added that if an inquiring slave owner was willing to agree not to act against His Majesty's interest in the future, he would be given permission to search the camp for his Negroes and take them if they were willing to go with him.

The sad truth was that most often enslaved people who escaped to the British gained at best unstable freedom. The British were not usually sensitive to the plight of black refugees. Life with the British brought new challenges. Refugees had to prove their value to the British war effort or be cast out. And they had to stay close to the British or risk being captured and sent back to slavery. In war's uncertainty and shifting circumstances, freedom remained a far-off dream for most enslaved blacks. Yet they lived on with hope that the British would one day bring the promised freedom.

CHAPTER

9

CLASH OF THE GENERALS

In late April 1781, General Lord Charles Cornwallis, second-in-command of the British army in North America, looked on as the first of fifteen hundred troops stepped off toward Virginia. Their stay in Wilmington, North Carolina, was at an end. After no word from his superior in New York, he had made the decision to head north, away from the main British base at Charles Town, South Carolina. He would meet up with the British troops in Virginia, under Phillips and Arnold. Someone had to move this war closer to an end.

Naturally aggressive, Cornwallis wanted to go out and fight. He did not want to wait for the rebels to come to him. Virginia was an attractive target for several reasons. It was the largest and most populous colony. And it was strategically important in several ways: Its deep harbors offered various ideal locations for a naval base, its farms provided a good source of food, and it bred some of the finest horses in the colonies. With additional horses he would be able to mount six hundred light dragoons and an additional seven hundred to eight hundred infantrymen, doubling his cavalry. Most important, though, many of the supplies streaming south to arm rebel troops came from Virginia. If he could disrupt or destroy this supply chain, he would directly help the British farther south. His efforts might be easier for two other reasons: Virginia was poorly defended, with militias that had grown complacent due to inactivity, and nearly 40 percent of its population was enslaved and would most likely not be voluntarily participating in the war.

General Charles Cornwallis's extensive military career took him all over the world, including North America, Ireland, modern-day Germany, France, and India, where he served as governor general and commander in chief.

Cornwallis, age forty-three, was a portly man with graying hair and a double chin. A sports injury in his youth gave his face a permanent somewhat quizzical look. Like Lafayette, Cornwallis came from a distinguished family and knew people in high places, namely King George III. As the family's oldest son, he had inherited the title of Earl Cornwallis in his early twenties at his father's death. With it came member-

This portrait shows General Henry Clinton in 1777, early in the American Revolution.

ship in the House of Lords, a position that outranked his commander General Clinton socially, but not in the military. Ironically, this man whose hereditary title earned him a great deal of respect in Britain mocked the vanity of titles and had no patience for pomp and fanfare. He tended to indulge his officers and troops to promote goodwill and unity, often at the expense of disciplining them, and as a result, his army was known for its bad behavior. But the troops loved him, and they were his family. He personally led assaults at the front of his army and, on the march, suffered alongside his men. He had demonstrated bravery on the battlefield and had even experienced several horses shot out from under him. If anyone could shake up Virginia, he could. Cornwallis was convinced that a successful battle in Virginia could bring an end to the war.

Sir Henry Clinton, Cornwallis's superior in New York and the top British commander in North America, had another idea. He was planning to direct Phillips south from Virginia to join Cornwallis in the Carolinas. Clinton was frustrated that Cornwallis had not communicated with him in almost four months. What was he up to? Before setting off for Virginia, Cornwallis had written to him, "I am very anxious to receive your Excellency's commands being as yet totally in the dark, as to the intended operations of the Summer." Cornwallis expressed his hope that the focus of the war would leave New York and move south to the Chesapeake Bay area. "Until Virginia is . . . subdued, our hold of the Carolinas must be difficult, if not precarious."

By the time Clinton had finally learned of Cornwallis's intentions, the troops were already on the move. In a letter, Clinton scolded Cornwallis: "I should certainly have endeavored to have stopped you . . . [I] consider such a move [to Virginia] as likely to be dangerous to our interest in the Southern Colonies." To Clinton's own boss back in Britain, he wrote, "My wonder at this move will never cease. But [Cornwallis] has made it, and we shall say no more but make the best of it." Virginians tended to be strong patriots. Virginia's representative to the Continental Congress, Richard Henry Lee, had been the first to call for independence from Britain. Clinton knew it was important to read the will of the people you were trying to conquer. He described the move into Virginia as a pointless endeavor if "we have not their hearts—which I fear cannot be expected in Virginia . . . we may conquer [but] we shall never keep."

Cornwallis and Clinton had a long and complicated relationship. Both had worked their way up in the British army and were highly trained officers. They were both veterans of military campaigns across Europe. Ever since he was a teenager, Cornwallis had been preparing for an army career. He attended military college and acquired his first commission as an ensign at age eighteen with the esteemed Grenadier Guards. Advancing quickly, he became a colonel and then a major general.

Sir Henry Clinton had become commander in chief of the British army in America in 1778, at age forty-eight. He had grown up in America, his father the royal governor of New York. He joined the army at age fifteen and at twenty-one was commissioned into the elite Coldstream Guards, but he later transferred to the Grenadier Guards, the most senior infantry unit in the British army.

Cornwallis had opposed British policies that led to the Revolution and as a member of the House of Lords had voted against the Stamp Act, a direct tax on goods in the colonies that was much hated. Clinton had not been enthusiastic about the war but was not opposed to British policies. Both were privately pessimistic about Britain's odds of military success in the long term.

When the American rebellion began, Cornwallis initially served under Clinton, beginning in 1776, and then under other leaders. By late 1778, he was fed up with the direction the war was going. Cornwallis resigned from the army and returned to Britain. His wife, Jemima, lay deeply ill in bed at their home in Suffolk. He raced to her bedside and stayed there until her death in February 1779. Distraught and aimless in the following months, he missed army life and decided to send a note to the king asking if he could rejoin the military. The king agreed. On April 4, 1779, Cornwallis wrote to Clinton, "This country [England] has now no charms for me, and I am perfectly indifferent as to what part of the world I may go." He hoped for a military

In 1780 and early 1781, British and American forces played cat and mouse across South Carolina and North Carolina. On August 16, 1780, Cornwallis annihilated American forces at Camden, South Carolina, a major triumph for him. On October 7, patriot militia forces won a victory at Kings Mountain, South Carolina, against loyalist forces. Next, in January, 1781, Americans defeated Colonel Tarleton at Cowpens, South Carolina. Two months later, in March, Cornwallis's troops clashed with Continental Army forces under General Nathanael Greene at Guilford Courthouse, North Carolina. It was a hard-fought battle, and Cornwallis lost many soldiers, but he managed a victory. He limped to Wilmington, North Carolina, on the coast, where his weary troops could rest and expect reinforcements and supplies from Charles Town.

post in the American South or the Caribbean. The military responded by offering him the position of second-in-command in North America, based in New York. He didn't really want to serve under Clinton, who he thought was a poor leader, but that was the offer.

"I am now returning to America," he wrote his brother William, "not with view of conquest and ambition, nothing brilliant can be expected in that quarter; but I find [England] quite unsupportable to me. I must shift the scene. I have many friends in the . . . Army." He returned to America in late July 1779 to work for Clinton in New York. Yet he soon became desperate for his own command again.

Clinton decided to launch a military campaign in the South and headed with Cornwallis to the largest Southern city, Charles Town. British troops surrounded the city, and it surrendered on May 12, 1780, a great victory. But a mutual dislike between Clinton and Cornwallis simmered beneath the surface. Cornwallis asked Clinton for a separate command. Since Clinton was eager to return to his base in New York City, he left Cornwallis in charge of Southern operations, with four thousand troops and a great deal of independence. It was just what Cornwallis yearned for: more freedom to make his own decisions.

After an almost 250-mile march, over dusty roads that wound past swamps and across creeks, Cornwallis's troops arrived in Petersburg, Virginia, just south of Richmond. General Phillips had died suddenly from his illness, and within ten days, Benedict Arnold received orders to return to New York City. Cornwallis immediately welcomed a new reality: He would be the sole decision maker in Virginia.

For now, Cornwallis had three goals: Hinder the colonists' ability to fight by destroying their military supplies, break the will of the people to fight, and wipe out Lafayette's army. His troops were seasoned, well disciplined, and agile. Cornwallis decided to send them into the interior of Virginia, away from the main waterways. They would live off the land, meaning off the food they stole from civilians. More Virginians were about to encounter the might of the British army.

This lithograph entitled *The Escape of Sergeant Champe* depicts John Champe being pursued by a British rider. It was published almost one hundred years after Champe escaped from the British.

Remember John Champe, the sergeant major recruited to capture Benedict Arnold in New York, who went undercover with the British army? After he was suddenly shipped to Virginia with Arnold before he could carry out his plan, he braved almost five months with the enemy before he found a safe moment to escape. At the time that Cornwallis joined Arnold's troops, Champe slipped away undetected and headed for the western mountains. He eventually ended up with his old Continental Army unit, who admired him for his daring adventure. Washington congratulated him, gave him a reward, and insisted on discharging him from service for his own protection. If the British had captured him, they would have hanged him.

Chapter

10

JEFFERSON ON THE RUN

Lafayette, the inexperienced general who had just arrived in Virginia, would now be fighting one of Britain's most experienced generals. On May 24, he wrote to Washington: "Was I to fight a battle I'll be cut to pieces, the militia dispersed, and the arms lost. Was I to decline fighting, the country would think herself given up. I am therefore determined to skirmish, but not to engage too far and particularly to take care against their immense and excellent body of horse whom the militia fears like so many wild beasts." Lafayette, expecting reinforcements from the North at some point, planned to shadow Cornwallis around the state and try to somehow stop or at least discourage him from doing whatever he wanted in Virginia. To be safe, Lafayette's troops needed to stay between twenty and thirty miles away from the British. If they got too close, the redcoats could launch a full-scale attack and wipe out his army. By staying in the vicinity, he could look for opportunities to pick off segments of the army.

Horses. The people of Virginia loved their horses. Horse racing was a huge sport, and Virginia was known throughout the colonies for its fine Thoroughbreds. Most farms of any size included horses. Cornwallis maintained a large cavalry, mounted troops that could ride quickly out front to gather intelligence, raid a plantation for supplies and food, and spread alarm throughout the countryside. A Virginia politician wrote to Washington: "By seizing the fine horses on James River, [the British] have mounted a gallant and most mischievous Cavalry of 5 or 600 in number."

That many men on horseback was intimidating, and the British knew it.

Cornwallis issued Rules of Engagement, General Orders, on May 28, 1781, stating that "to prevent the scandalous practice of taking Horses from the Country people [Virginians]," officers should issue receipts and make payments based on the individual's "past and future Conduct." In other words, they could take horses from patriots and loyalists, but they should reimburse the loyalists. They wanted to keep loyalist support, after all.

Conversely, Lafayette's major weakness was lack of cavalry troops. His army had only a few dozen mounted soldiers. A cavalry could travel far and fast and was the eyes and ears for a general. Without one, Lafayette often didn't know the location of his enemy. He wrote to Washington that "we have everything to fear from their cavalry." In desperation, Lafayette asked Governor Jefferson for permission to seize horses from Virginia citizens. The law allowed Jefferson only to authorize Lafayette to confiscate horses within twenty miles of the army. Lafayette wrote, "We are in the utmost want of Cavalry; the Enemy's great superiority in Horse giving them such an advantage over us that they have it almost in their power to over run the country in spite of all of our efforts." In another letter, the Frenchman complained that "all the fine horses in the country are falling into the enemy's hands . . . this will in the end prove a ruin to this state."

Seizing a person's horse was a delicate task. As the enemy, the British didn't mind making rebels mad. However, Americans seizing horses from their own citizens could turn people against the patriot cause. It was a delicate problem, and Lafayette learned to assign his most diplomatic officers to the task of appropriating horses. Virginia law eventually supported this effort.

☆ ☆ ☆

Cornwallis's most valuable fighting unit was his British Legion, made up of American loyalists under the command of a young British officer, Lieutenant Colonel Banastre Tarleton. The twenty-six-year-old had earned a reputation in the Carolinas for being a fierce fighter and a terrifying force to avoid. Stunning in their green uniforms, his men were known as Tarleton's Raiders. He'd been in America since December 1775 and had worked with Cornwallis early in the war.

Banastre Tarleton was the third of seven children born into a family in Liverpool in Britain. His grandfather was a ship owner and slave trader.

In his youth, Tarleton had planned to become a lawyer, but he ended up buying a position as an officer in the army at age twenty-one. At the time, men could pay money to secure a leadership position in the British army.

Tarleton's Raiders brought widespread destruction wherever they went, causing all kinds of trouble for civilians. Tarleton boasted that he would "carry the sword and fire through the land." Cornwallis wanted to destroy the will of the people to fight, and Tarleton was his not-so-secret weapon. Tarleton's dragoons, as they were also called, charged through the countryside looting and burning the plantations of patriots and loyalists alike, driving those with loyalist tendencies to the patriot side.

Cornwallis first decided to dislodge Lafayette from the

This image depicts a man named Peter Francisco fighting Tarleton's cavalry in Virginia. He stood six feet, eight inches tall and was called the Virginian Giant or Virginian Hercules, well-known for his size and strength. He fought with the 10th Virginia regiment in many battles of the war. In what was later called Francisco's Fight, he claimed to have fought off a band of Tarleton's Raiders singlehandedly when they tried to arrest him and take his silver shoe buckles.

Richmond area, only to discover the American troops had already left. On May 15, Lafayette had ordered his troops to evacuate Richmond, and Governor Jefferson and the General Assembly fled west toward Charlottesville, sixty miles away, a government on the run. Lafayette's men had moved munitions supplies to the foothills west of Richmond.

So British troops headed north toward Fredericksburg, a town with an iron foundry and small-arms factory, crucial to

Virginia's war effort. The cavalry was soon causing much alarm throughout central Virginia. Cornwallis had his army on the move constantly, keeping the rebels off-balance. He issued this order to his cavalry: "All public stores of corn and provisions are to be burnt, and if there should be a quantity of provisions or corn collected at a private house, I would have you destroy it." He anticipated that the crops would otherwise be appropriated by the Americans and shipped south to help the rebel cause there. Virginia militia leader George Weedon wrote to Lafayette on June 4 that the enemy's superior cavalry allowed it to "range about the country as to dismay the people not a little and keep them in continual alarm for the safety of their families." Lafayette already knew this all too well.

In Hanover County, the British cavalry ransacked the home of the recently widowed Elizabeth Clay and her four-year-old son, Henry (future Speaker of the US House of Representatives from Kentucky, presidential candidate, and US secretary of state). The cavalry pillaged the house, shattered furniture, took food and liquor, and destroyed clothing including Elizabeth's wedding dress. The British also reportedly desecrated the graves of her husband and mother with their bayonets and took many of the family's slaves with them.

But then, Cornwallis changed his mind and decided to stop his march north. An attack on Fredericksburg would be easier by water, from the Rappahannock River, so he would save that for the navy. Instead, after causing major destruction in central Virginia, his troops would next head west toward known weapons stores and the tantalizing target of the Virginia legislature and Governor Jefferson, who were reconvening in Charlottesville.

No portrait of Eliza Ambler is known to exist, but this portrait depicts her sister, Mary, called Molly, who was one year younger. After the war, Mary married a young man named John Marshall, who would one day be chief justice of the US Supreme Court.

One Virginian caught in the chaos and forced to run was sixteen-year-old Eliza Ambler from Yorktown. Her father was treasurer of the Virginia government. They had moved to the capital, Richmond, and dealt with the British invasions there. She wrote in her diary: "What an alarming crisis this is! War in itself however distant is indeed terrible, but when brought to our very doors, the reflection is overwhelming."

Eliza then fled Richmond and headed for Charlottesville with her father, invalid mother, and younger sister, Molly, age fifteen. Her family was trying to avoid the roving British cavalry as it terrorized the countryside. In her diary, Eliza penned an entry in the form of a letter to her friend Mildred Smith, who lived in Yorktown. "The nearer the mountains the greater the safety, was the conclusion; so, on we traveled through the byways and brambles until we could get to the main road leading to Charlottesville. Our design was first to reach a plantation in the neighborhood of the Springs, where we were at least sure of house, room, and a bed; and to this place we proceeded, where we arrived just as the sun appeared in all his glory. With difficulty we got admittance, no soul being in the house, and were just spreading pallets to rest our weary heads, when the landlord, out of breath, reached the house, saying that Tarleton and all his men had just passed, and would catch the Governor before he could reach Charlottesville. What a panic for us all!"

☆ ☆ ☆

Governor Thomas Jefferson was on the run. What a prize he would be for the British! He was governor of the largest colony and author of the Declaration of Independence. But a man named Jack Jouett happened to be at the Cuckoo Tavern in Louisa County, forty miles east of Charlottesville, when a group of British soldiers came in. Overhearing their talk and guessing they were headed to capture Jefferson, he snuck out of the tavern and rode his horse hard on back roads, through the night, to warn the governor. Jouett coaxed his horse up a steep hillside, branches slapping his face, until he reached Jefferson's home, Monticello, at 4:30 A.M. and pounded on the door. Jefferson reacted calmly to the news and woke his wife and two daughters, and his guests including Thomas Nelson Jr., the commander of the militia, and Speaker of the House

Jefferson's estate Monticello, meaning *little mountain* in Italian, sits high above Charlottesville, Virginia. He designed the famous domed house, drawing from various architectural styles.

Martin Hemings was a member of an enslaved family of almost seventy people who lived at Monticello over five generations. Jefferson inherited them from his father-in-law. The sparse historical record leaves few clues to Martin's life. At seventeen, Martin sold Jefferson a mockingbird for a family pet. It was the first in a series of singing birds that were part of the household. He became butler at age nineteen and served for twenty years. Martin was twenty-six when the British invaded Monticello. Hemings could read and write and do math sums and was entrusted with making purchases for the Jefferson family.

Benjamin Harrison (whose family portraits had been burned by the British). They were all in grave danger.

Jefferson bundled his family into a coach and sent them on their way, headed south. The guests made an unwise decision to return to Charlottesville, where the legislature was meeting. Unwise because Tarleton had decided to search for Jefferson there first. Upon arrival, he ordered his troops to block the roads and search the buildings one by one for the governor.

Meanwhile, Jefferson wanted to make certain the news was correct. He grabbed a telescope and rode to an adjacent higher mountain that afforded a clear view to Charlottesville. He glimpsed columns of dragoons moving down the streets. He raced back to the home he had spent almost twelve years designing. What important papers should he take with him? He knew that Tarleton's men had been burning homes across the state. He stuffed papers into his saddlebags, mounted his horse, and rode off, not knowing if he would have a house to return to.

Less than five minutes later, several of Tarleton's men rode up the drive, pointed a gun at one of Jefferson's enslaved butlers, Martin Hemings, and demanded to know where Jefferson was. Hemings refused to tell them. They searched the house, found some of Jefferson's fine wine, and helped themselves. After an eighteen-hour stay, they left, without disturbing anything else.

While Monticello escaped destruction, Jefferson's Elk Hill plantation twenty-nine miles away, toward Richmond, did not. Little did Jefferson know that at the moment he was fleeing Monticello, Cornwallis's seven thousand troops were camped out in Elk Hill's corn and tobacco fields for ten days, helping themselves to whatever food they could find, including the livestock. Cornwallis himself lived in the farmhouse, identifying his location in his correspondence as "Jefferson's Camp." The British destroyed the property, ruining the corn and tobacco crops, burning all the barns and fences, and killing all the remaining animals. During the British stay, twenty-three of Jefferson's enslaved people escaped to the enemy. Jefferson and his family, traveling separately, remained on the run for ten days, making various stops and reuniting farther west at his Poplar Forest plantation.

Tarleton's dragoons stayed a day in Charlottesville and then left. They had captured seven members of the Virginia legislature, including frontiersman Daniel Boone (a delegate from a far west county in present-day Kentucky), but Jefferson had

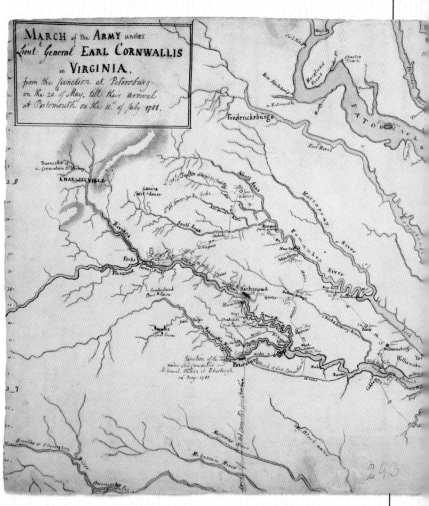

This British map from 1781 highlights the movement of Cornwallis's troops in red ink and lists the dates at each location from late May to early July.

escaped. Cornwallis was disappointed. After destroying one thousand muskets, four hundred barrels of flour, uniforms, and some tobacco and county records, Tarleton's Raiders and Cornwallis's troops headed east to where their navy could support them.

Lafayette's army was about fifty miles east of Charlottesville, waiting to connect with Wayne's force coming from Pennsylvania. The Frenchman was relieved that the British were turning around. Lafayette wrote, "Virginia is not conquered and the American army . . . is not annihilated." Yet, the British continued to hold the state in its grasp. They still controlled the waterways and the entrance to the Chesapeake Bay from the Atlantic Ocean, still outnumbered the American troops in strength, and still maintained a large cavalry. An aide to Lafayette told the Virginia General Assembly that Lafayette's cavalry had sixty horses while the British had five hundred. The Continental forces desperately needed support from the Virginia militia if they were to have any chance of combating the British, but recruitment in the militia was inconsistent. Men in some of the western counties were refusing militia service, while others around the state were joining the militia, outraged at the British atrocities they'd seen.

Everyone had the same big question: Where would the British strike next?

CHAPTER

11

WAYS TO FREEDOM

Lafayette was desperate for more soldiers. He wrote to the new governor, Thomas Nelson Jr., to express concern about the shortage of men available to fight. Recruiting enslaved black Virginians to fight seemed an obvious solution to the manpower shortage. If they would be guaranteed their freedom at the end of the war, that would be a powerful incentive. Virginia law forbade arming the enslaved, but free black men could use firearms. Lafayette may not have known that James Madison, future author of the US Constitution and future president, was among those people who had already proposed that the enslaved be allowed to serve in Virginia's military. Madison wrote, "Would it not be . . . well to liberate and make soldiers at once of the blacks themselves?" Such a policy "would certainly be more [consistent] to the principles of liberty which ought never be lost sight of in a contest for liberty." Despite this and other calls, the Virginia legislature, made up of many slave owners, refused to consider the idea.

The French general knew that black men were fighting in the Continental Army in the North. They had fought with the militias at the first battles of the war: Lexington, Concord, and Bunker Hill. When the Continental Army had formed in 1775, it excluded black men from enlisting because a central military needed to reflect the opinions of all the states, and some states were against arming them. But free blacks wanted to serve, and General Washington advocated for the reenlistment of those who had already served prior to the existence of the Continental Army. Congress approved this request.

As the war continued, Washington faced an extreme shortage of soldiers in his Northern army. This scarcity gradually encouraged black recruitment in the North, with states such as Rhode Island taking a lead. One of Washington's aides, and a friend of Lafayette's, became an unlikely and highly vocal advocate for recruiting the enslaved. John Laurens had grown up in a slave-owning family in South Carolina. His father had been a slave trader and later served as president of the Continental Congress. Educated in Switzerland and England, John returned to America with a zeal not only to fight against Britain but to free slaves. Abroad he had made British friends who had convinced him that slavery was immoral; he saw military service as a way to offer enslaved men freedom.

When British leaders planned a Southern campaign and troops occupied Savannah, Georgia, in 1778, Congress decided to approve the recruitment of slaves in South Carolina and Georgia. It recommended that the states "take measures immediately for raising three thousand able-bodied negroes." They would form into separate battalions, each battalion commanded by a white officer. Slave owners would receive financial compensation. Black soldiers would receive no pay for their service, but they would receive clothes and food at government expense. Provided they served "well and faithfully" to the war's end, they would receive freedom and a small amount of money.

That was the plan; however, it was met with opposition. Congress asked John Laurens to travel south, to his South Carolina homeland, to build local support for the plan. But the state's governor, John Rutledge, and legislature quickly dismissed the idea.

The Rhode Island legislature passed an innovative law in February 1778 that permitted the enlistment of able-bodied African Americans and Native Americans, both free and enslaved, in a new regiment, the 1st Rhode Island. An enslaved person accepted into the regiment agreed to serve in the Continental Army for the entire war and at war's end would be "immediately discharged from the service of his master or mistress, and be absolutely free."

Like Virginia, South Carolina was a large slave state, importing two thousand slaves a year over a twenty-year period. Laurens vowed not to give up. He wrote to his good friend and fellow Washington aide Alexander Hamilton that he would not stop his efforts to fight for black soldiers "while there remain the smallest hopes of success."

By the summer of 1778, the Continental Army included a number of black soldiers, many in New England units, despite the comparatively small black population in the region. The First Rhode Island Regiment enrolled close to two hundred free black men and became known as the Black Regiment. In some cases, the state had purchased a man's freedom from his owner and then promised the man his freedom at the end of the war.

Denied black soldiers in Virginia, Lafayette raised the possibility of recruiting a force of 150 black men to march with the army, in a supporting role, as wagoners to work with moving freight. He needed to find a way to make use of any person willing to join the patriot effort. It shouldn't matter the color of their skin.

CHAPTER

12

MARCHING TO NEW YORK

COUNT DE ROCHAMBEAU
French General of the Land Forces in America Reviewing the French Troops

This mocking British cartoon from 1780 shows General Rochambeau reviewing his troops.

On June 10, Rochambeau at long last led the French forces out of Newport and headed toward the Continental Army encampment near Philipsburg (now Hartsdale), New York. (See map on pages 22-23.)

It was a colorful sight. In their brilliant white uniforms, the four thousand soldiers marched two by two, the column stretching for miles through the green countryside: four groups of a thousand each, leaving over four consecutive days. The French leaders, engineers, and cartographers had carefully planned and marked the route of march through Rhode Island and Connecticut. They set up supply depots along the way and established designated campsites with easy access to clean water. Each day, forty-three hundred men would wake at 2:00 A.M., begin marching by 4:00 A.M. to avoid the heat of the day, and cover twelve to fifteen miles.

Rochambeau rode at the head of the first regiment, the Bourbonnais. At the front of each regiment was a group of workmen commanded by an engineer. They monitored road conditions and cleared the way, filling in potholes and removing obstacles like fallen trees. Officers led the troops, followed by horse-drawn artillery (mobile field cannons), seven wagons of Rochambeau's baggage, and wagons carrying officers' luggage and tents. Each soldier wore a white wool uniform, gaiters (a cloth or leather piece wrapped around the lower leg and boot), a powdered wig, woolen underwear, and a tricorn hat with black trim and a white, red, and black cockade. He carried equipment weighing almost sixty pounds, including a musket.

Following next were wagons with medical supplies, wagons carrying chests of money, and wagons loaded with supplies and equipment for butchers and bread makers, and then brigades of support personnel like wagonwrights and blacksmiths. Finally, there were wagons carrying fodder for the animals, with the livestock bringing up the rear. Rochambeau's staff also included ten or so servants, some free, some enslaved.

Each night, the procession set up camp, tents stretching along the road for nearly three miles. The local inhabitants had never seen anything quite like this before. The march was an opportunity for ordinary American citizens and French soldiers to assess each other. No one really knew how the general American public would react to having French soldiers on American soil. The last time it occurred, during the French and Indian War decades earlier, the French were the enemies.

They were now allies, and many locals greeted the French with thanks for their help in the battle for independence. Almost every evening featured music and dancing. In Woodbury, Connecticut, a man named Daniel Sherman held a party with lively music and served apples and eight barrels of apple cider. July 1 was General Rochambeau's fifty-sixth birthday, and their final night in Connecticut. His

This is a portrait miniature of the Comte de Lauberdiere. Miniatures were usually painted to mark a milestone in the person's life and given to close friends and family. In this case, Lauberdiere may have given it to a family member in France when he embarked for America.

staff held a celebratory fête, and General Washington sent an aide to attend it.

The Americans made a good impression on the French, who appreciated American hospitality. The comte de Lauberdière, Rochambeau's twenty-one-year-old nephew, served as one of the general's aides and translators. He kept a diary of his war years, often describing the landscape and people he encountered. He wrote, "The entire country from Providence to the North River differs very little . . . it is very wooded, full of hills, boulders and ravines. It abounds in pastures and cattle, especially Connecticut. The inhabitants are fairly brave and good soldiers. Patience is one of their virtues."

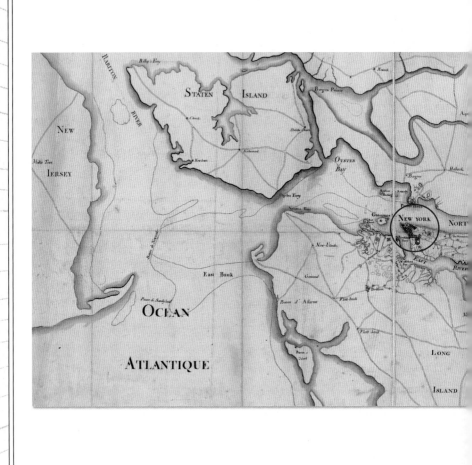

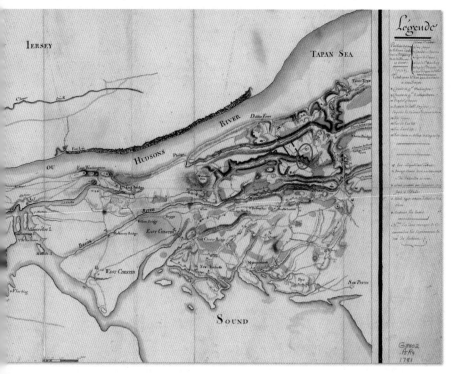

A map showing the position of the combined allied armies—American and French—in Philipsburg, New York, on the eastern side of the Hudson River. Look for the British base on the left (red circle), today's Manhattan. At the far right (blue circle), you can see Washington's and Rochambeau's headquarters. Louis Alexandre Berthier, a soldier in Rochambeau's army, drew the map, one from a series of at least 111 beautifully detailed maps of places the French army went.

And the Americans could not help but be impressed with the French troops. They warmly welcomed their French saviors. An article in the *Connecticut Courant* (now the *Hartford Courant*, America's oldest continuously published newspaper), stated: "A finer body of men were never in arms, and no army was ever better furnished with everything necessary for a campaign. The exact

This sketch of American soldiers was drawn at Yorktown by French officer Jean Baptiste Antoine de Verger, who served under Rochambeau. It includes a black member of the 1st Rhode Island regiment and is one of the earliest images ever found depicting an African American soldier.

discipline of the troops, and the attention of the officers to prevent any injury to individuals, have made the march of this army through the country very agreeable to the inhabitants, and it is with pleasure we assure our readers that not a single disagreeable circumstance has taken place." A New Yorker later wrote in his journal: "We now greet [the French] as friends and allies, and they manifest a zealous determination to act in unison with us against a common enemy."

After marching across Connecticut, they arrived at their destination at Philipsburg, New York, on July 6. The comte de Lauberdière wrote, "General Washington's demonstration of joy upon seeing us join him was very moving." Washington gave an official welcome, expressing his thanks to "his Excellency the Count de Rochambeau for the unremitting zeal with which he has prosecuted his march in order to form the long wished for junction between the American and French forces." And, according to Lauberdière, the French once again indulged in military spectacle: "our troops . . . appeared in the grandest parade uniform. M. de Rochambeau took his place in front of the white flag of his oldest regiment and saluted General Washington . . . Our general received the greatest compliments for the beauty of his troops." The French military leadership thus far had had limited interaction with their American counterparts and were curious to meet them.

The following day, the Americans invited the French officers to observe the American army. The French were shocked at what they saw! Baron von Closen, Rochamebeau's aide, wrote, "I had a chance to see the American army, man for man. It was really painful to see these brave men, almost naked with only some trousers and little linen jackets, most of them without stockings, but would you believe it? Very cheerful and healthy in appearance. A quarter of them were negroes . . . confident, and sturdy . . . Three quarters of the Rhode Island regiment consists of negroes, and that regiment is the most neatly dressed, the best under arms, and the most precise in its maneuvers." A French officer, Jean-François Louis de Clermont Crevecoeur, wrote, "In

On his first night in New York, Crevecoeur was in his tent in the middle of a field, trying to fall asleep. He suddenly noticed hundreds of small flashes of light flying over the grass. Was it sparks from a fire somewhere? Was there danger? On further inspection, much to his delight, he identified small flying bugs that glowed. They were magical and lit up the night. He knew glowworms back home, but these fireflies, as the Americans called them, were new to him.

beholding this army, I was struck, not by its smart appearance, but by its destitution: the men were without uniforms but covered with rags; most of them were barefoot. They were of all sizes, down to children, who could not have been over fourteen. There were many negroes, mulattoes, etc. Only their artillerymen were wearing uniforms. These are the elite of the country and are actually very good troops, well-schooled in their profession. We had nothing but praise for them later."

Rochambeau's headquarters was only three-quarters of a mile from Washington's. They still had not reached an agreement on their upcoming target and would soon have to decide: New York City or Virginia.

CHAPTER

13

THE TOWN OF YORK

As he continued his raids into the Virginia heartland, Lord Cornwallis began to realize that he was fighting a losing battle. Admiral Thomas Graves poetically described British movement in America as "the passage of a ship through the sea whose track is soon lost." The British leaders were trying to destroy the will of the people to fight, but it didn't seem to be working. They were failing to gain support from any remaining loyalists (those who had not left). The rebel militias were becoming more active, no doubt driven by revenge for the personal destruction. And Lafayette continued to fly around him like an annoying gnat. Cornwallis took to referring to him as "the boy." The British general had been a soldier for as long as Lafayette had been alive. Despite Lafayette's noble background, Cornwallis had little respect for this young, inexperienced foe. Should he try to lure Lafayette into a major battle? Cornwallis needed a bigger plan of action.

In early July, Cornwallis received new orders from Clinton in New York. Based on intelligence from his spies and on the French army's move to New York State, Clinton was feeling more vulnerable and was convinced that an attack on his stronghold was in the works. He ordered Cornwallis to establish a defensive post in a healthy and strategic location in Virginia, keep the troops necessary to defend it, and send three thousand troops to New York. This annoyed Cornwallis. Clearly, Clinton did not share his belief that Virginia was the key to subjugating North Carolina and western South Carolina.

Cornwallis decided to set a trap for Lafayette. The transport ships sat at Portsmouth, so Cornwallis needed to move troops there. The march would require crossing the James River, a two-mile effort. The Americans knew that any time an army crossed a wide body of water, the men tended to spread out and were vulnerable. Cornwallis sent only his baggage and some cavalry ahead across the river to make it look like the main part of the army had already crossed. Then, the British concealed themselves, lying in wait to surprise the Americans, who would assume the rear was exposed.

Suspicious, Lafayette went ahead to investigate. He spotted the hidden British troops, but too late to warn his advance force under General Anthony Wayne. They walked into the trap and barely escaped, managing to retreat before dusk (today the encounter is referred to as the Battle of Green Spring). It was quickly becoming dark, and Cornwallis chose not to pursue them but instead continue to Portsmouth. Soon after, Lafayette wrote, "This devil Cornwallis is much wiser than the other generals with whom I have dealt. He inspires me with a sincere fear, and his name has greatly troubled my sleep. This campaign is a good school for me, God grant that the public does not pay for my lessons."

The dispatches from Clinton started coming at a rapid rate, one after another, dated different times, often not in the order they were written. Cornwallis was getting very frustrated. Clearly, Clinton was receiving mixed messages from his intelligence analysts and advisers, causing him to keep changing his mind. The troops had already started loading the transports for the journey to New York when a new order arrived: Cornwallis was to keep all troops in Virginia and call back any that had shipped out. He was to locate a place on the York River that could be fortified and used as a naval base for the lower Chesapeake Bay.

If a Virginia campaign was to succeed, it would need support from the Royal Navy. The base would need to be defensible and have a deep harbor and area for large ships. Clinton was planning a large expedition up the Chesapeake Bay in the fall. He didn't like Portsmouth for two reasons: It was a confined area and had an unhealthy climate. Clinton preferred Old Point Comfort in Hampton or Yorktown, but he would let Cornwallis choose. Cornwallis just wished Clinton would make up his mind!

After visits to several potential sites, Cornwallis concluded that Yorktown was the only place with a harbor best suited to his needs. It would require a major effort by the army to build the necessary fortifications. This was no small task. Still, Yorktown was an excellent trade port, with easy access to the Atlantic Ocean and locations around the Chesapeake. With naval support, it was a site he could defend. He wasn't planning on the need to guard it beyond the normal requirements of a naval base. The decision was final. Orders went out telling his scattered troops: Evacuate Portsmouth, converge on Yorktown.

Brigadier General Charles O'Hara, new British commandant of the Portsmouth garrison, had a problem. He was having a hard time dealing with the rampant disease that was raging through the troops and camp followers, including the many escaped slaves who had come seeking freedom.

A View of the Town of York, Virginia, from the River

This watercolor shows the town of York as seen from the York River in 1755.

As early as June, Cornwallis had recommended that all soldiers and army support staff be inoculated for smallpox, a highly contagious disease easily spread through contact with an infected person. Furthermore, soldiers were to avoid interaction with former slaves who had not been inoculated. Smallpox became an increasing problem, and American soldiers found the British route littered with sick and abandoned black refugees. Some American officers accused the British of intentionally leaving them there to spread smallpox to the Americans. The ugly scene unnerved all who encountered it. For the sick, medical attention was in short supply.

In early August, when O'Hara was ordered to oversee the evacuation of Portsmouth, he asked Cornwallis what to do with the many hundreds of black refugees who were sick and dying. He didn't have the capacity or orders to evacuate them from

Portsmouth. But he hardly wanted to leave them there without support. "They would inevitably perish if our support were withdrawn from them." He decided to break open the army's stores, so they would at least have some food.

Cornwallis replied to O'Hara, "It is shocking to think of the state of the Negroes, but we cannot bring a number of sick and useless ones to [Yorktown]. Some flour must be left for them and some people of the country appointed to take charge of them to prevent their perishing."

O'Hara responded that they were forced to abandon more than four hundred black refugees, mostly women, children, and older people, passing them to the Norfolk side and begging the locals to take them. The British left only fifteen days' worth of provisions.

Cornwallis's focus was now on Yorktown. York, as it was then known, was described by a French traveler as "a very pretty little town inhabited by some of the [most refined] people in Virginia, who have some very pretty buildings here." It was a thriving port town of two hundred or so buildings, where goods arrived from all parts of the world: rum, medicines, and textiles. It included Grace Church, Swan tavern, and a brick courthouse. Its busy waterfront featured storehouses and businesses, with wharfs running into the river. Much of the town's wealth had come from tobacco, and stately homes of wealthy merchants lined the streets of the upper town on the bluffs. One of the prominent features of its skyline was a windmill, used for grinding corn into meal and wheat into flour. It stood at the edge of a steep bluff; its sails easily seen from the river. The main road to

Williamsburg, twelve miles away, ran west in the middle of the peninsula. Hampton Road led southeast to Hampton, roughly eighteen miles distant.

The people of Yorktown had seen British soldiers before. The enemy had come raiding earlier that year, in April, and Cornwallis had personally surveyed the town for a possible naval port in late June. When the troops showed up to stay in August, many of the townspeople moved out.

Thomas Nelson (known by the nickname "Secretary"), sixty-five, uncle of the Virginia governor, decided to stay. He was quite comfortable in his large, two-story mansion with four massive chimneys, located at the highest point in town. He had maintained a close relationship with the royal governor Dunmore, having served on the governor's council for more than thirty years. He had even helped the Dunmore family escape from angry patriots. Lord Cornwallis promptly occupied Nelson's home and made it his headquarters. Though loyal to Virginia, Nelson figured that if Cornwallis lived there, his house might be safe from attack. Then again, it might become a target. He never dreamed he would soon be in the center of a battle!

Cornwallis estimated it would take his troops and fifteen hundred to two thousand black laborers about six weeks to build defense works. Yorktown occupied low, sandy hills that an enemy could attack from several directions. From the north, Gloucester Point sat a half mile across the York River. Cannons placed there could easily reach town, so the point would need to be occupied by Cornwallis and defenses built there. West of town, a swampy area formed a natural barrier between the town and a high ridge along the river. South of town posed a bigger problem, since it was wide-open, mostly level ground that would need to be defended. East of town was the river and Wormley Creek. The southern approach would need the most protection.

The general's land forces numbered about 8,885, supplemented by another 840 sailors. He was not worried about Lafayette's troops. The commander initially thought that after digging defenses at Yorktown, most of his men would relocate to New York, leaving a smaller army to guard the base. This vision of the future all changed when enemy sails were spotted on the bay.

CHAPTER

14

DECISION AT LAST

General Lafayette found it difficult to keep track of Cornwallis's activity. Was he staying in Portsmouth, was he preparing to head back south, or north to New York? Lafayette needed to know more. He decided to increase his intelligence operation. He ordered Colonel James Innes, a graduate of the College of William and Mary in Williamsburg, to set up a broader spy network. Innes bought provisions for his spies and sent them out as tradesmen selling goods. He was authorized by Lafayette to pay any person who could prove he had been in a British camp, and to offer more money for significant information.

Lafayette was also relying on James, the enslaved man he had recruited. All spies working undercover have a cover story, the background information they offer the people around them who ask probing personal questions. James's cover story is not known. Was he an escaped slave? A free black? The British soldiers may have wondered what he thought of the rebellion. Did he have an answer? Or perhaps they ignored him as long as he did what they requested.

Like the other spies, James would have known that the more invisible he was, the better. He must have found ways to slip in and out of the British fortifications at Portsmouth. He may have started going there as early as May, when Benedict Arnold was commander, but certainly by late July he was a familiar sight in camp. But he wasn't who the British thought he was.

In this letter from Lafayette to General Washington dated July 31, 1781, many historians believe James was "the correspondent." Lafayette always began his letters to Washington with "My dear General."

Lafayette was careful never to mention James or any other spy by name in his correspondence.

On July 31, 1781, Lafayette wrote to Washington, likely referring to James:

> A correspondent of mine, servant to Lord
> Cornwallis, writes on the 26th of July, at
> Portsmouth, and says his master [Cornwallis],
> [and] Tarleton, . . . are still in town, but expect
> to move. The greatest part of the army is
> embarked. My lord's baggage is yet in town. His
> lordship is so [secretive with] his papers that my
> honest friend says he cannot get at them. There
> is a large quantity of negroes, but, it seems, no
> vessels to take them off . . . I shall take care at
> least to keep [the British] within bounds.

James, a servant to Cornwallis? He had found a way into headquarters? Somehow, James must have earned Cornwallis's trust . . . to a degree. Clearly, the general kept his papers locked up from prying eyes. Still, James was able to report thirty transport ships of British soldiers, eight to ten brigs with cavalry on board, and a forty-four-gun ship. Cornwallis was on the move, and Lafayette needed to find out where he was headed.

In mid-July, Cornwallis had declared that the role of orderlies (a person assigned to perform various chores for an officer) was to be filled solely by blacks. Perhaps James had found this kind of job. If he stayed in British headquarters, working in some capacity, James could overhear conversations and, in rare moments, peruse any documents or maps lying around. The

British had little reason to suspect a slave of working for Lafayette. They had seen many enslaved people eager to gain freedom with the British, not the Americans.

James was most likely part of a growing network of spies who worked together, a chain of people who could deliver messages to Lafayette. He may have worked with Saul Matthews, another enslaved man serving as a soldier and spy for his owner, Thomas Matthews of Norfolk County. Saul accompanied Thomas into the army when he enlisted and carried out several missions into the British fortifications at Portsmouth. He scouted out the enemy's position and guided a group of men from the Fifth Virginia Regiment behind enemy lines, where they captured some British guards. On several occasions, Saul delivered vital information about British movements to American leaders. Whatever their secret techniques, Saul, James, and others had to be very careful not to get caught with incriminating evidence in their possession. The result would be immediate death.

In New York City, one big question was on General Clinton's mind: Was the target for the Americans in 1781 New York or Canada? He didn't realize that Virginia was an option. Some said the Americans were definitely planning an attack on New York City. Others said an attack on British troops in southern Canada was in the works. With the French army's move to the New York region, it looked increasingly likely that the city was the target. But to Clinton's great frustration, he kept receiving mixed messages from his spies. Both Washington and Clinton maintained intelligence networks throughout the New York area to track enemy activity.

James Moody, a farmer in New Jersey, was a loyalist who had refused to swear allegiance to the patriot cause. He had fled to the British military and fought in several battles, eventually ending up in service intercepting rebel correspondence. His familiarity with the northern New Jersey landscape helped him to predict the routes that couriers often used to deliver messages between Washington and Congress. His gang of men worked to capture mail, while the local militia worked to capture them. His efforts eventually became known to Washington, who called him "that villain Moody."

In early June, Moody had arrived at General Clinton's headquarters in New York City with a bundle of thirteen letters he had confiscated in the hills of New Jersey. British intelligence experts immediately examined them and certified their authenticity. The British were cautious of planted misinformation in the mail, a practice both sides used. Clinton was so overjoyed with the letters that he rewarded Moody with a cash award on the spot. They were letters from Washington to Congress and to Lafayette describing his recent meeting with Rochambeau in Wethersfield. As one British soldier who observed the encounter later wrote, "The capture of this mail is extremely consequential, and gives the Commander in Chief [Clinton] the most perfect knowledge of the designs of the enemy."

In one of the letters, Washington had written to a general named Sullivan about his meeting with Rochambeau. In it, Washington said that while he saw advantages to following Sullivan's plan to attack Canada, there were some big hurdles in obtaining men, transportation, and supplies that made it less preferable than New York.

In the letter to Lafayette, Washington had written, "An attempt on New York with its present garrison . . . was deemed preferable

to a Southern operation as we had not the command of the water."
While the letter raised a Southern option, it also dismissed the idea.

How could analysts ensure the letters were authentic? In this
case, they were confident in the validity of these letters in part
because the bundle included a letter from Washington to his dentist in Philadelphia requesting dental tools: a pair of pincers to
fasten the wire of his teeth and some scrapers to clean his teeth.
He mentioned he would not be in the city any time soon. This
seemed to indicate the letters were valid because if Washington
were traveling south, he would most likely go through Philadelphia and could meet with his dentist. They concluded that Washington wasn't planning to head south.

Both sides worried about intercepted mail. Clinton in New
York and Cornwallis in Virginia kept in touch through enci-
phered letters sent by messengers in small unmarked boats. The
Americans, British, and French all used cipher codes. For example, the Pig Pen cipher replaced certain letters with symbols on
a grid. Both the sender and receiver needed to know the code in
order to read it. If the receiver did not know the code, he was
out of luck. Both sides changed the various cipher codes on a
regular basis. Once, British correspondence fell into American
hands and a cryptology expert, who happened to be a member of
the Continental Congress, decoded it and determined the British
were still using the same cipher he had cracked previously.

For now, Clinton felt pretty confident that the American target was going to be New York City.

☆ ☆ ☆

It was past time for Washington to decide whether to target New
York or a place in Virginia. Canada was never really a serious

New Windsor May 29th 1781

Sir,

A day or two ago I requested Col. Harrison to apply to you for a pair of Pincers to fasten the wire of my teeth. — I hope you furnished him with them — I now wish you would send me one of your scrapers, as my teeth stand in need of cleaning, and I have little prospect of being in Philadelphia soon. — It will come very safe by the Post — & in return, the money shall be sent so soon as I know the cost of it. —

I am Sir
yr. very Hble Servt.
G. Washington

The British had to determine whether this captured note from Washington to his dentist in Philadelphia was authentic. It is now part of the General Henry Clinton papers at the University of Michigan library.

option and had been dismissed months before. In order to make a wise decision, the allied leaders needed solid, up-to-date intelligence. To get a better sense of the British army's strength, Washington, Rochambeau, and French military engineers carried out a Grande Reconnaissance, a three-day tour close to the British lines. In person, they assessed the British fortifications and encampments on the northern end of Manhattan, ten miles from Philipsburg, staying far enough away to avoid any confrontation with the enemy. It was the first real test of whether or not they could work well together. Just days earlier, Washington had told Rochambeau that the target remained New York. But after gaining a clearer picture of the enemy's assets, Washington began to change his mind. On August 1, with the reconnaissance complete, Washington wrote: "I could scarce see a ground upon which to continue my preparations against New York, and therefore . . . I turned my views more seriously . . . to an operation to the Southward."

Rochambeau and Washington were waiting, once again, to hear from a French military official. This time the official was Admiral de Grasse, the naval commander in charge of the large fleet in the West Indies. Rochambeau had been promised his aid. Finally, on August 14, a courier arrived at Rochambeau's New York headquarters with a letter from de Grasse. The French general notified Washington, and they anxiously read the letter together. De Grasse was headed for the Chesapeake! Rochambeau was thrilled. "I shall be obliged to employ the fleet promptly and to good purpose," de Grasse wrote, "so that the time may be spent to profit sufficiently against the enemy naval forces and their land forces; but I shall not be able to use the soldiers long." De Grasse's expected arrival in the Chesapeake was two weeks hence. Twenty-eight ships of the line! Combined with the various support vessels, the armada would be much larger than anything the British could organize. De Grasse was also bringing more money that Washington desperately needed to pay his troops. In addition, Admiral de Barras, commander of the French fleet still in Newport, would join in the attack with men and the heavy artillery siege guns they hadn't bothered to transport to New York.

To Rochambeau, it seemed like the decision had been made for them. Yet diplomacy was important in this moment. Rochambeau knew that Washington had to feel like the decision was his. While Rochambeau had

Admiral de Grasse had a long and distinguished naval career, beginning at age seventeen when he officially entered the French Navy. Six months after Yorktown, he suffered a humiliating defeat to the British navy in the Caribbean and was taken prisoner to London.

placed the French army under Washington's command, he had to remind the American general that de Grasse and the French navy were not. Still, Washington had to make the final decision regarding the army's movements. He dreaded a long march from New York to southern Virginia, and even his former aide Alexander Hamilton predicted Cornwallis would get wind of the venture and escape into North Carolina.

What Rochambeau hadn't told Washington was that before he left Newport, the French commander had written to de Grasse to send him a summary of the Wethersfield, Connecticut, conference with Washington. He told de Grasse that the situation in Virginia was getting worse. He feared that Cornwallis might attack Lafayette's small army. He suggested that if the combined armies in the North could march south, with support from the French navy, they could surprise Cornwallis. Rochambeau later recalled, "I then suggested, as my own opinion, the [suitability] of attempting an expedition to Chesapeake against the army of Lord Cornwallis, and which I considered more practicable," adding that "it will be there where we think you may be able to render the greatest service." This seemingly played a part in influencing de Grasse's decision.

While the decision may have seemed obvious to Rochambeau, to successfully implement a Southern attack would require many complicated parts. It was one of the weightiest decisions that Washington would have to make during the war. To a degree, his hand had been forced. An attack on New York would be impossible without support from a strong navy, and the only navy available was the French one . . . and it was headed to Virginia. In addition, Washington's chief military engineer submitted a report estimating that a minimum of twenty thousand soldiers would be necessary to take New York. They had nine thousand. Washington had written to Congress and the state governors begging for more troops. None had come.

As Washington agonized over the decision, a dispatch arrived from Lafayette. The Frenchman wrote that he had been receiving conflicting information about British movement from his spies and for a while could not tell where the main army would settle. But then his intelligence began pointing to Yorktown. He reported that the enemy was digging in on the bluffs of the York River. Lafayette's excitement was obvious: "Should a [French] fleet come at this moment, our affairs would take a very happy turn." Washington couldn't believe his good fortune. He knew

Yorktown and the surrounding landscape well; it was only a dozen miles from Williamsburg, the former capital of Virginia, where he had visited and worked often. In 1777, an officer had suggested Yorktown as a good place for a small base to monitor the movement of the enemy's ships. But Washington didn't think it was a good idea, warning that "by being upon a narrow neck of land, [the troops] would be in danger of being cut off." With a French naval blockade and artillery surrounding the town on land, Cornwallis would be in that danger. Surrounded, he would be forced to surrender. Washington now knew his plan, describing the moment later "as clear to my view as a ray of light."

The next day, August 17, Washington sat at his desk and wrote to Admiral de Grasse: "We have determined to remove the whole of the French army and a large detachment of the American army to the Chesapeake to meet your Excellency in Virginia." Both Washington and Rochambeau signed it and sent it by a stealthy network of couriers. Fast ships sped it to de Grasse.

The decision was made at last! Together with the French navy, the American and French armies would mount the largest coordinated operation of the war. Armies would march over hundreds of miles; navies would sail over hundreds of miles. Everyone's focus was now one place: Yorktown, Virginia.

☆ ☆ ☆

Once the plan to entrap Cornwallis at Yorktown was put into motion, Washington was nervous that the British general would somehow get wind of it and escape south before the allied troops could arrive. Washington wrote to Lafayette, "I hope you will keep Lord Cornwallis safe without provisions or forage until we arrive. Adieu."

Lafayette ordered several detachments to guard possible escape routes. He also recognized it was now time to use another spy technique: planting false information in Cornwallis's camp.

Lafayette recruited Charles Morgan, called Charley, a member of a New Jersey brigade and one of the boldest spies of the war. He had been a farmer in Monmouth County, New Jersey, before the Revolution. He agreed to pose as a deserter, telling the British that he had enlisted to fight under Washington but refused to serve that Frenchman Lafayette. He would trick Cornwallis into believing that Lafayette had enough boats at the ready to move his troops across the James River in three hours. He was instructed to exaggerate the number of boats available to Lafayette, so that Cornwallis would decide that marching the army south to North Carolina was not a good idea. Charley followed the plan and was convincing enough that he found himself talking to Cornwallis and Tarleton themselves! Cornwallis asked him if Lafayette had enough boats for the entire American force. Charley replied that he did. Morgan then had to find a way to escape back to the Americans.

A short time later, Morgan shocked Lafayette and his officers by appearing at their headquarters—Lafayette saw six British soldiers and a Hessian waiting for him. Morgan, wearing the British red uniform, had persuaded five British soldiers and a Hessian soldier to desert with him. Charley Morgan was the talk of camp, and his fame spread. Like Champe, the American soldier who had pretended to desert to the British in an attempt to capture Benedict Arnold in New York, Charley had been worried about the disgrace of people thinking he had deserted. He had made a deal with Lafayette that if he were somehow caught and hanged by the British, Lafayette promised to clear his name by publishing the truth in a New Jersey newspaper. Of course, Lafayette wanted to promote him for his bravery. But Charley wasn't interested; the only reward he wanted was the return of his old musket.

On August 25, Lafayette wrote to Washington.

> The enemy have abandoned their forts at Ivy, Kemp's Landing, Great Bridge, and Portsmouth. Their vessels with troops and baggage went round to York [Yorktown] ... I have got some intelligences by the way of this servant I have once mentioned [probably James] ... from him as well as deserters I hear that they begin fortifying York. They are now working by a windmill at which place I understand they will make a fort and a battery for the defense of the river. I have no doubt but that some things will be done on the land side ... The enemy have 60 sails of vessels into the York River the largest a 50-gun ship, two 36[-gun] frigates and seven other armed vessels. The remainder are transports some of them still loaded and a part of them very small vessels. It appears they have in that number merchantmen some of whom are Dutch prizes. The Men of War are very thinly manned. On board the other vessels there are almost no sailors. The numbers of the British army fit for duty I at least would estimate at 4500 rank and file.

While Lafayette's spies watched the dirt fly at Yorktown, the pressure was on. Cornwallis could not get wind of this grand plan. Clinton in New York could not either.

CHAPTER

15

THE BIG SECRET

General Washington was suddenly faced with putting together a giant jigsaw puzzle. For the plan to work, he had to ensure that all the pieces fit into the right spots in the right order. He and Rochambeau had to move some seven thousand troops five hundred miles over land and water and keep it a secret from the British as long as possible. (If a city, the camp would have been the sixth largest in America at the time!) A camp of thousands would require hours to assemble and get moving each day, plus food not only for the people but also for the thousands of animals traveling with it. It also left a significant imprint on the land, clues for the many British spies swarming across the area. How could they possibly keep this a secret?

Washington needed to get the allied troops away from the New York area before Clinton realized what was happening and could attack. The line of march would be spread out and vulnerable. Secrecy was crucial because if the allies got far enough, to Pennsylvania, the British couldn't catch up and prevent them from going to Virginia. Washington also had to decide how many Continental troops to keep at West Point, to secure this American stronghold protecting traffic on the Hudson River.

For its part, the French navy sailing from the Caribbean needed to arrive, deliver troops, and block the entrance of the Chesapeake Bay to ensure that Cornwallis in Yorktown couldn't receive any supplies or reinforcements. De Grasse could stay in Virginia only six weeks before he had to return to the West Indies.

In addition, the French fleet in Newport needed to deliver the French heavy artillery at just the right time. Meanwhile, Lafayette and his troops in Virginia would have to monitor Cornwallis closely and somehow keep him from escaping over land before the American army could surround him.

Since Clinton assumed that Washington was planning to attack New York City, the American commander decided to reinforce that assumption by feeding Clinton disinformation that would make him keep thinking this. Clinton's spies continued to deliver intelligence that Washington was active in the area. Since one avenue of attack could be Staten Island from the southwest, any troops marching south did not immediately suggest they were headed for Virginia.

Washington wrote afterward that "much trouble was taken and finesse used to misguide and bewilder Sir Henry Clinton in regard to the real object, by fictitious communications [letters], as well as by making a deceptive provision of ovens, forage and boats in his neighborhood." Because the plan was so secret, Washington told only top officers. Dr. James Thacher served with the Continental Army as a surgeon and kept a detailed journal during the war. He wrote, "Our destination has been for some time a matter of perplexing doubt and uncertainty; bets have run high on one side, that we were to occupy the ground marked out on the Jersey shore, to aid in the siege of New York, and on the other, that we are stealing a march on the enemy, and are actually destined to Virginia, in pursuit of the army under Lord Cornwallis."

Washington used a variety of deception strategies to keep the secret.

One involved planting false communications. Washington ordered a mail courier named Montagnie to travel a route vulnerable to mail interception. Sure enough, the British captured him and the mail. The fake letters indicated that New York City was the target. Washington also sent road repair crews to fix specific roads that led the British to assume a certain direction of attack. The Americans fed misinformation to British spies, too, attempting to make the army appear larger than it was. This would make the British more cautious.

Another deception related to the well-known French love of bread. Wherever their army and navy traveled, they were sure to have fresh bread in their diet. French warships included large ovens to bake bread. The army built brick bread ovens wherever they were camped for a period of time. Washington wrote in his diary: "French bakery to veil our real movements and create apprehensions for Staten Island." The comte de Lauberdière provided more detail, writing, "But to assure that our movements were not interrupted, we had to give the enemy a diversion and to make them fear for New York. Mr. de Villemanzy, Commissioner of War, was charged with making a bakery at Chatham in the Jerseys with great preparation and fanfare but at the least expense."

By building fake bread ovens, the French tricked the British into thinking they were staying in the area for a longer period. French buyers went into the New Jersey countryside to purchase flour, and builders searched for bricks to construct the ovens. Rochambeau even had troops guard the fake ovens! One of Washington's aides wrote in his journal on August 21, "French ovens are building at Chatham in [New] Jersey. Others were ordered to be prepared at a place near the Hook [Sandy Hook, New Jersey]."

Washington also directed carpenters to build more than thirty boats on the Hudson River and mount them on carriages to transport them to the necessary location. This only confirmed Clinton's suspicions that the army was planning a water assault on either New York City or Staten Island. It would take many boats to move soldiers across the water surrounding Manhattan. But Washington had no actual use for these boats. It was a ruse.

Since the British assumed the French fleet would show up at some point, Washington played to this assumption by making it look like preparations were underway for the arrival of the fleet. He wrote, "Contracts are made for forage to be delivered immediately to the army on their arrival at the last-mentioned place. Here it is supposed that batteries are to be erected for the security and aid of the fleet, which is hourly expected. By these maneuvers and the corresponding march of the troops, our own army no less than the enemy are completely deceived."

On August 19, with no fanfare due to the secrecy surrounding the mission, the combined American and French troops began the long five-week march south. They would not all arrive at their destination until September 26. Along the route, various units would split up and move at different paces. It was a complicated movement of men, animals, and heavy equipment. The two forces spoke different languages. Boats needed to be at the ready; river crossings were especially hazardous, whether moving men or weighty cannons. Quartermasters continually scoured the countryside to feed the hungry soldiers.

Washington continued to keep their destination a secret from many officers and all enlisted men. The comte de Lauberdière provided the reason: "Calculating people [and] indiscreet tongues are not rare in the army. It was essential to throw them off track. Everybody believed that the purpose of the maneuvers they observed was the siege of New York."

Washington sent spies into New York to find out if his deception was working. It was. So the commander in chief began calling on troops from Delaware and Pennsylvania to prepare to join the march.

Once in New Jersey, the Americans and French split up and followed parallel paths south, to confuse the enemy about the size of the force. The columns extended up to three miles and included a combined total of more than four thousand horses and oxen. Each mile of troops included about 125 wagons loaded with all kinds of supplies. They needed food, water, and a place to rest each night. A soldier's rank dictated his type of lodging. Officers slept in nearby homes or taverns, while their men slept in tents. On a good day's march, they covered fifteen miles. To avoid the hottest part of the day, the troops were usually on the march by 4:00 A.M. and walked twelve to fifteen miles to the next campsite.

On August 27, Washington wrote to the deputy quartermaster, Samuel Miles, in Philadelphia to start assembling boats at Trenton. The boats would transport troops down the Delaware River. "I have delayed having these preparations made until this moment, because I wished to deceive the enemy with regard to our real object as long as possible, our movements have been calculated for that purpose and I am still anxious the deception should be kept up a few days longer, until our intentions are announced by the army's filing off towards the Delaware [River]." As soon as British spies noticed a lot of activity near Trenton, on the river not far northeast of Philadelphia, they would get suspicious.

★ ★ ★ ★ ★ ★

Map of
ALLIES' MARCH

✶ ✶ ✶ ✶ ✶ ✶

On August 19, 1781, the combined, or allied, American and French armies began a secret march from their New York camp heading south on a mission to entrap General Cornwallis at Yorktown, Virginia. The Allied leaders tried to keep it secret as long as they could, though moving thousands of soldiers, animals, and supplies over hundreds of miles proved a huge challenge. To confuse the British, the armies separated into two groups in New Jersey and again in Maryland, where some of the troops traveled by ship, the rest over land.

MAP KEY		
▭ Allied Camp	0 50	
– – – – Water Route	**MILES**	
– – – – Land Route		

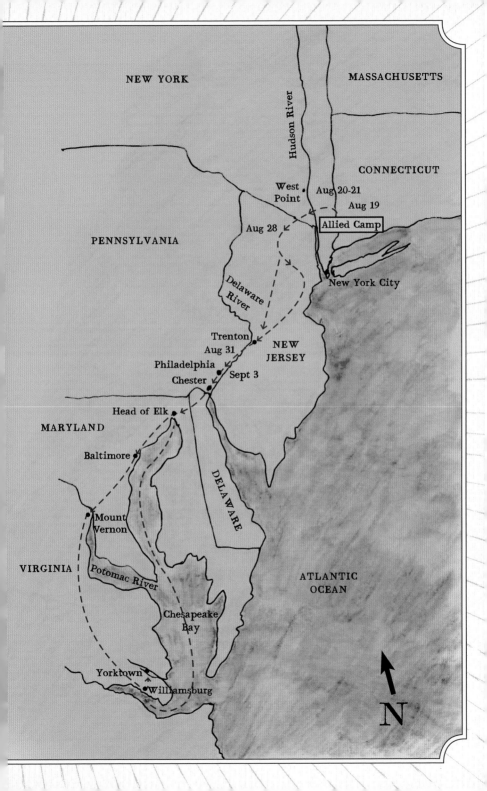

NEW YORK

MASSACHUSETTS

Hudson River

CONNECTICUT

West Point

Aug 20-21

Aug 19

Allied Camp

PENNSYLVANIA

Aug 28

Delaware River

New York City

Trenton

Aug 31

NEW JERSEY

Philadelphia

Chester

Sept 3

Head of Elk

MARYLAND

Baltimore

DELAWARE

Mount Vernon

VIRGINIA

Potomac River

ATLANTIC OCEAN

Chesapeake Bay

Yorktown

Williamsburg

N

the State House

The East Prospect of the City of PHILA

The September 1 *Pennsylvania Packet* reported, "Yesterday, at one o'clock in the afternoon, His Excellency the Commander-in-Chief of the American armies, accompanied by the Generals Rochambeau and Chastellux . . . arrived in Philadelphia." Philadelphia, the largest city in the states and seat of the Continental Congress, had a population of just under twenty-five thousand. It featured a university, a hospital, Protestant and Catholic churches, a Jewish congregation, and wide streets with sidewalks, lined with brick houses.

The militia light horse met the generals on the city's outskirts and escorted them to City Tavern, where Washington received several visitors. He next went to the house of the superintendent

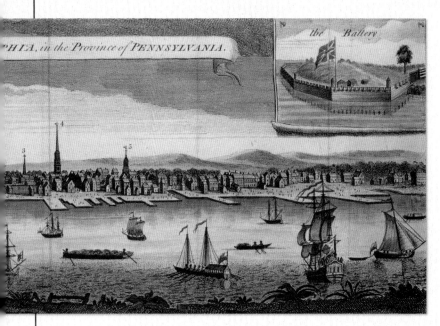

the Battery

'HIA, in the Province of PENNSYLVANIA.

The French soldiers who passed through Philadelphia in 1781 saw a thriving city with busy wharves on the Delaware River. This image shows the city as portrayed in a London magazine in 1761.

of finance, then to the State House to pay his respects to Congress. The *Packet* reported, "After dinner, some vessels . . . fired salutes to the different toasts which were drank. In the evening the city was illuminated, and his Excellency walked through some of the principal streets, attended by a numerous concourse of people, eagerly pressing to see their beloved general."

If the city of Philadelphia was excited to see Washington and Rochambeau arrive, it was even more excited to see the American and French troops arrive over the following days. They entered the city with drums beating and flags waving. The crowds cheered and "were absolutely amazed to see such a fine army," wrote the French officer Crevecoeur, referring to the French troops. They marched past the State House, where Congress had signed the Declaration of Independence, and a reviewing stand filled with members of Congress along with Washington and Rochambeau. The French army camped a mile from downtown on the Schuylkill River. The city put on a grand illumination that night as well, lighting candles in many windows and featuring parades of boys with torches. With all the public spectacle, there was no doubt the British leadership now knew the secret.

Lauberdière wrote, "Mr. Clinton believed so much that [the allies] had come to attack him, he was far from imagining that we were going two hundred and fifty leagues farther, that he crossed 2000 men to Staten Island to oppose the Americans. He was not the only one who made false assumptions about the allied army when it began to march. *Secretum meum mihi* [my secret is mine], that is Mr. de Rochambeau's great principle in war."

Heading south from Philadelphia, Washington and Rochambeau continued ahead of the troops, trying to prepare the way. They separated temporarily, Washington leaving first. He had hoped to hear news that the French fleet had reached the Chesapeake while the armies were still in the vicinity of New York more than a week earlier. He was becoming increasingly anxious when no word came, especially since he received reports that the British navy in New York had set sail, headed south. If the British reached the Chesapeake before the French fleet, the current plan wouldn't work: The enemy would control traffic on the bay. Washington wrote to one of his generals that "the present time is as interesting and anxious a moment as I have ever experienced." Where was the French navy? "I am almost all impatience and anxiety at the same time," Washington wrote to Lafayette.

Rochambeau took a boat down the river to Chester, a town

south of Philadelphia, to meet up with Washington. He wanted to travel by water to see some old forts on the river. As his boat approached the shore, he saw a very tall American officer waving his hat and twirling a white handkerchief over his head. He was shouting something, but Rochambeau couldn't understand. This person was exuberant about something!

When he reached the dock, he realized it was Washington, "waving his hat at me with demonstrative gestures of the greatest joy." De Grasse had arrived in the Chesapeake with twenty-eight ships of the line. The French now controlled the entrance of the bay. Washington embraced Rochambeau in a big hug. A French officer, the duc de Lauzun, later wrote, "I never saw a man more thoroughly and openly delighted than was General Washington at this moment."

Washington quickly shared the news with the troops, and word made it to Philadelphia, where crowds cheered in the street and ran to the residence of the minister of France and shouted, "Long live Louis the Sixteenth!" To encourage his officers and troops, General Washington wrote an announcement: "The General calls upon the gentlemen officers, the brave and faithful soldiers he [has] the honor to command, to exert their utmost abilities in the cause of their country, to share with him . . . the difficulties, dangers and glory of the enterprise." Lauberdière wrote, "From this moment the goal, the purpose of the march was no longer a secret. Everyone forgot past hardships in the hope of an imminent and brilliant future."

While victory was far from assured at this moment, a big piece had been fitted into the puzzle. Without the French navy, the entire effort would have failed. But with the French navy in control of the bay, Cornwallis was stuck. He could not receive reinforcements

or supplies of food or ammunition. He was trapped on a peninsula, surrounded, as long as Lafayette and his army could hold him
there. Still, until the allied troops could arrive and the extra French
soldiers with the navy could disembark, the numbers still favored
the British.

Washington and Rochambeau had no idea how long Cornwallis could hold out, and Admiral de Grasse had been very clear
that he only had a specific window of time until he needed to
return to the West Indies. The armies had to get to Yorktown
quickly. The race was on! Baron von Closen wrote in his journal:
"One must not count his chickens before they are hatched." And
Washington could not forget that piece of intelligence he had received about a British navy heading for the bay. Depending how
large it was, it could cause big problems. At this point, nothing
was certain.

King Louis XVI, only three years older than Lafayette, ascended
to the throne in 1774.

CHAPTER
16

BATTLE AT SEA

Descended from one of the oldest families in France, François Joseph Paul, comte de Grasse, had a reputation for being demanding and impulsive. His flagship, the *Ville de Paris*, named for the city that had funded it, was the largest French warship on the seas.

On August 30, his fleet of twenty-eight ships of the line and five frigates sailed into the Chesapeake Bay. They saw no sign of the British navy, but de Grasse expected to see them any day. Near Jamestown, he began unloading thirty-two hundred soldiers from bases in the West Indies. He positioned ships of the line at the bay's entrance, sending frigates to patrol the water farther out to provide alerts for any sign of the enemy.

The comte de Grasse did not have long to wait. At 10:00 A.M. just six days later, on September 5, lookouts spotted large ships heading their way. At first, de Grasse hoped it was Barras coming from Newport, but he quickly realized it was the enemy.

Rear Admiral Thomas Graves was in command of a British fleet of nineteen ships of the line and eight frigates, a collection of ships from the West Indies and New York. Five of them were in poor fighting condition. However, all of them had copper keels, making them faster, sturdier, and better able to repel cannonades. Only 50 percent of French ships were coppered. Graves was shocked to see the French blocking his way. He was doubly surprised at the size of the French fleet, since he had expected it to be much smaller than his own. Nevertheless, he began preparations for battle.

" ENGLAND~"
Nelson's Famous Signal
616

Ships of every size used colorful signal flags arranged
in different patterns to communicate messages.

Ships in a fleet communicated with one another through
colored flags raised in different patterns. Navies created special books
listing these codes, which were top secret. If the French were able to
read the Royal Navy's signals, they could anticipate how the British ships
would maneuver, giving them an advantage. Historians think the New York
publisher of the loyalist newspaper the *Royal Gazette*, James Rivington,
was a spy for the Americans. Somehow, Rivington managed to obtain a
copy of the Royal Navy's codebook and pass it to de Grasse. The historical
evidence suggests that de Grasse had the book, but it remains somewhat
mysterious to this day.

The French sailors were watching, and all signs from the British pointed to an impending battle, so de Grasse raised the signal flag to prepare for a fight. Captains cried, "Up all hammocks!" Sailors hung hammocks, yards, and nets in place to catch splinters and falling men. Gun crews ensured that powder and balls were at hand. Crews sprinkled sand on the decks to provide traction and absorb a mess of blood. Despite the tide moving in the wrong direction, de Grasse was impatient. The French crews heaved their anchors and sailed out to meet the British. The mouth of the bay was ten miles across at its widest point, but the boat channel was only three miles wide. It would take a while to get into line for battle, the *Ville de Paris* in center position. Maneuvering into a line of attack took about ninety minutes. They were ready by 3:45 P.M., nearly six hours since the French first spied the British sails.

At 4:15, the British opened fire, with Rear Admiral Graves at the center of the British line in the *London*. The British began with a wind advantage, but by 5:00 P.M. the wind had shifted in favor of the French. The British were outgunned, their 1,500 cannons to 2,000 on the French side. Soon into the battle, three British ships were damaged and forced to leave the line, while others received major topsail damage. The heroic ship of the day was France's 80-gun *Auguste*, which reportedly fired 654 cannon shots during the battle. It pounded HMS *Terrible* into a floating wreck.

After roughly two and a half hours of fighting, darkness approached and the British ceased firing. Almost a third of the British and French lines had never engaged, being too far apart. Both sides began work on repairs, though the French ships had received relatively little damage. De Grasse had high hopes of

This image captures the drama of the Second Battle of the Capes, also called the Battle of the Chesapeake, and depicts the massive ships in line of battle formation engaged in a fierce fight.

continuing the battle with an even better position the following day, if the British did not slink off in the night. While de Grasse's first priority was keeping control of the bay, he entertained thoughts of a more decisive outcome in which his fleet damaged more British ships.

In the following days, the enemies jockeyed for position in the wind, with Graves trying to steer clear of an attack and continuing to make repairs. The *Terrible* was so badly damaged that Graves made the decision to sink it. But it refused to sink. So the British set it on fire and burned it. The two fleets remained in sight of each other, out of sight of land for the next few days; but it soon became clear that the British were in no condition to reengage. Graves called a council of war and concluded that "upon this state of the position of the enemy, the present condition of the British fleet . . . and the impracticality of giving any effectual succor [help] to Lord Cornwallis in the Chesapeake, it was resolved that the British squadron . . . should proceed with all dispatch to New York, and there use every possible means for putting the squadron into the best state for service." The British limped away to New York, thus ending what would be called the Second Battle of the Capes. Cornwallis would get no help from the Royal Navy.

On September 19, Admiral Graves reached New York after his disastrous encounter with the French navy. Six days later, Admiral Robert Digby arrived in New York with three British ships of the line. It brought the total number to twenty-five. The ship carpenters worked long hours to complete repairs on Graves's damaged ships, since Clinton had promised to help Cornwallis. Amid the tension, the citizens of New York were clamoring to get a glimpse of the first member of the British royal family to visit American shores. Sixteen-year-old Prince William Henry, third son of King George III (who later became King William IV), was serving as a midshipman to Digby. Clinton had to entertain the young prince, not something he wanted to do at the moment. His worry was that the repairs would not be completed in a timely manner.

It would take more than a week for news of the French navy's victory to reach Washington and Rochambeau. Meanwhile, the big swarm of humans and animals, the city on the move, continued its slow journey south, through Delaware. The quartermasters and purchasing agents continued to scour the countryside buying food. Washington sent letters to the leaders in the states along the march asking for their help with procuring provisions and livestock. The Americans had no money, which forced them to pay with IOUs, while the French paid in silver and gold coins. This became a problem because what farmer would not prefer to be paid in silver or gold? In some cases, the Americans found themselves competing with the French for food. As they moved into Virginia, food became scarce. The British already had been there and had scavenged the land. Seventeen days' worth of provisions per man consisted of a pound of cheese, a little rum, and a package of biscuits.

The quartermasters tried to locate meat to supplement the diet. Outdoors, food—and especially meat—spoiled easily. Often people preserved meat by salting or smoking it, but the army preferred to have a drove of cattle accompany the army and to slaughter the animals at various points.

Wherever possible, Washington moved troops on waterways.

Water transportation was always cheaper and faster than land transportation since roads were usually in horrible condition. Freight companies charged ten times more for overland transport than for water transport. The goal had been to transport as many soldiers as possible by water, from Head of Elk, at the top of the Chesapeake, down the bay to Williamsburg. It soon became clear that there were not enough boats available for use locally. The British in their various raids in Virginia had destroyed many of them. More soldiers than planned would have to walk the entire way south, past Baltimore and Annapolis in Maryland. A small number of transports from de Grasse's fleet eventually came to pick up some of the troops and artillery, but many soldiers would be walking.

Along the way, states added to the army's numbers. Three new Maryland regiments numbering eighteen hundred men joined the march.

As Washington traveled through Maryland, he was again ahead of Rochambeau by a day. He rode hard, covering 120 miles in two days. He had a renewed incentive to move fast: He was nearing Virginia and his home, Mount Vernon. The general hadn't been home in almost six and a half years, since the start of the war. His wife, Martha, was there, along with four grandchildren he'd never met, born since the war began. After a sweet reunion with his family on September 9, and an inspection of the property, he prepared for the arrival of his special guest. The following day, Washington welcomed Rochambeau. He entertained the French general that evening with a sumptuous feast, proud to show off his estate and introduce him to Martha and the rest of his family. It impressed one of Washington's aides, who wrote, "An elegant seat and situation; great appearance of opulence and real exhibitions of hospitality and princely entertainment." But they could not stay long. They left at 5:00 A.M. on Sept. 12 and rode together to Dumfries, then on to Fredericksburg, where Washington's mother, sister, and brother-in-law lived.

Washington knew Virginia's roads and rivers well. He had traveled to Williamsburg many times as a member of the House of Burgesses, the legislative body in colonial Virginia. He passed near many places that held deep personal meaning for him: the plantation where he had courted Martha, the church where they had been married, homes of friends where he had spent pleasant evenings visiting and dancing. His homeland had been invaded by the enemy. In many ways, the fight had become very personal for him. His state was suffering, and he was finally here to try to save it.

On the evening of September 14, Washington and Rochambeau arrived in Williamsburg, the staging area for their armies. General Lafayette had been anxiously awaiting this moment for a long time. A witness described the exuberant reunion. "the Marquis, riding [at] full speed from the town [Williamsburg] . . . approached General Washington, threw his bridle on his horse's neck, opened both his arms wide as he could reach, and caught the General around the body, hugged him as close as it was possible, and . . . kissed him from ear to ear once or twice . . . I was not more than six feet from the memorable scene."

Over the next couple of weeks, the officers, troops, and sections of the wagon train arrived in Williamsburg. The duc de Lauzun and his mounted hussars (cavalry) boarded boats at Head of Elk to travel down the Chesapeake Bay, where they hit bad weather. Lauzun later recalled that they "embark[ed] on all sorts

This colorful painting shows Washington (*front*) and Lafayette at Yorktown with cannonballs scattered on the ground. It is an example of an artistic style called folk art, meaning it was painted by an untrained artist.

of boats . . . the boats were awful, two or three turned over, and we had seven or eight men drowned." After a brief stop in the Annapolis area, they returned to the boats for ten more days, continuing to face bad weather.

Admiral de Grasse's official notification to Rochambeau about his victory over the Royal Navy arrived in Williamsburg on September 14, the same day that Rochambeau and Washington arrived. They were thrilled with this news! Washington immediately wrote de Grasse: "I take particular satisfaction in felicitating [congratulating] your Excellency on the glory of having driven the British fleet from the coast and taken two of their frigates. These happy events, and the decided superiority of your fleet, gives us the happiest presages of the most complete success in our combined operations in this bay." The French now controlled the entrance to the Chesapeake Bay and access to Yorktown by water. On his return to the bay after the battle, de Grasse was surprised to see that Admiral de Barras had arrived from Newport with crucial pieces of heavy artillery. His ships had snuck by during the standoff between the navies. With both French fleets now at hand, all the naval pieces of the puzzle were now in place.

Yet de Grasse began to get impatient to return to the West Indies. It was hurricane season, and he feared potential destruction should one sweep in from the sea. Rochambeau and Washington were desperate to keep the navy in place, because its absence would leave the allies vulnerable. The British navy might return from New York to aid Cornwallis. It was time to pay a visit to de Grasse on the *Ville de Paris* (the admiral never left his flagship the entire time he was in the Chesapeake).

On September 17, Rochambeau and Washington, along with some aides, traveled several hours into the bay to the French armada. Washington had never been among such a powerful sea of masts: three dozen ships of the line, gleaming fortresses on the water, complex and beautiful. With their towering sails and intricate rigging, they each held between 60 and 120 cannons on two or three decks. One American soldier described them: "The most noble and majestic spectacle I ever witnessed."

Washington was impressed, grateful, and elated; the months of planning were coming together, and de Grasse had made everything happen. The fleet was dressed with flags, and Washington and his entourage climbed aboard to a thirteen-gun salute. It was a meeting of the big men: De Grasse was as tall or taller than Washington, who stood at six feet two inches tall. He gave the American general a big bear hug and kisses on both cheeks (called *bises* in French). Then, in keeping with his loud and

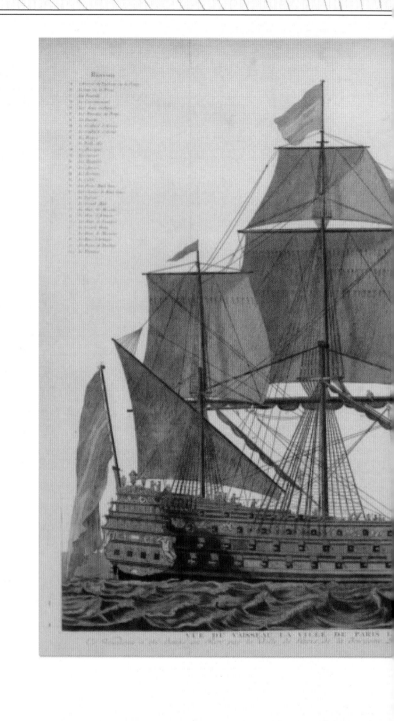

VUE DU VAISSEAU LA VILLE DE PARIS

De Grasse's flagship, the *Ville de Paris*, pictured in 1764. The ship had 104 guns on three levels. Less than a year after Yorktown, she was captured by the British in battle and sank in a hurricane off the coast of Newfoundland.

self-assured personality, he shouted, "Mon cher petit général!" (My dear little general!), to the merriment of all. That night, de Grasse's crew served the important visitors a large feast, and all of them drank to the health of King Louis XVI, Congress, and the commanders. The comte de Grasse then gave Washington a tour of the flagship. At 177 feet long, with 104 cannons on three decks, it was a floating castle.

Washington waited for the right opportunity and then raised a matter of business. Would de Grasse be willing to extend his stay by two weeks, until October 30, to give Washington extra time if it was needed? No one knew how long it would take for the siege to force Cornwallis to his knees. De Grasse, convinced by Washington's argument, agreed and offered another two thousand men for the fight. Washington wrote to Philadelphia: "I am happy to inform Congress that I found the French Admiral disposed in the best manner to give us all the assistance in his power and perfectly to co-operate with me in our present attempt."

As the sun set that evening, the French troops activated a *feu de joie* (fire of joy), a rifle salute performed by soldiers on ceremonial occasions. It created a spectacular show to honor the commanders. On every mast in the fleet, sailors lined the yards and tops, each one firing in succession along the ranks to make a continuous sound and puffs of smoke in a pattern. Washington and Rochambeau left de Grasse's ship feeling confident.

CHAPTER

17

CORNWALLIS DIGS IN

Throughout August, Cornwallis's troops had been digging in at Yorktown, building trenches and defense structures for their big guns. They cut down trees and demolished a few buildings that were in the line of direct fire. With this transformation, the location would be a safe place for the Royal Navy to harbor, perhaps over the coming winter. Everyone moved slower than usual due to the heat and humidity. "For six weeks the heat has been so unbearable that many men have been lost by sunstroke or their reason has been impaired. Everything that one has on his body is soaked from constant perspiration. The nights are especially terrible, when there is so little air that one can scarcely breathe," wrote one officer. On many days, officers declared it too hot for their men to work. Instead, they had the work taken up by many former slaves who had taken refuge with them. These men struggled and strained to alter the landscape. Cornwallis knew his troop size was larger than Lafayette's, and so he was in no danger of an attack. He concentrated on construction, oblivious to the forces moving toward him.

However, Cornwallis's confidence decreased rapidly on August 30, when lookouts spotted French warships: first, several at the mouth of the York River, seven miles away, then an armada of thirty or forty at the entrance of the bay twenty miles distant. After that, the French landed three thousand troops only fifteen miles from Yorktown. They were fresh from the West Indies, troops Cornwallis was not expecting. The British general became alarmed. The Royal Navy was supposed to keep French ships away.

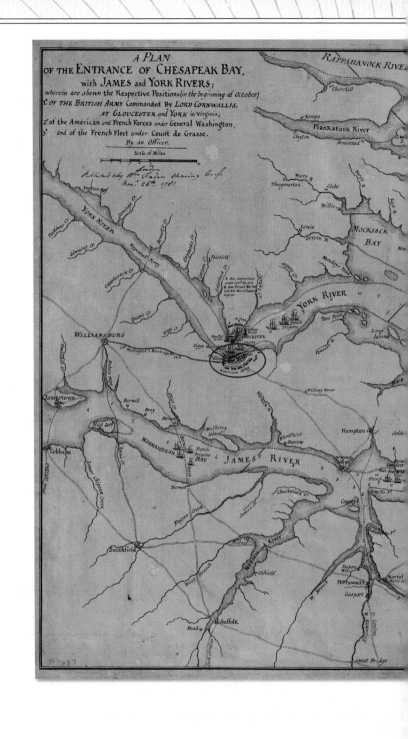

BAY

OF

CHESAPEAK

Point

Haven

Fort

French Fleet under Count de Grasse thirty two ships of the Line

at Singly Anchor

Cherrystones

CAPE
CHARLES

Smith Island

THE MIDDLE GROUND

THE HORSE SHOE

LYNHAVEN BAY

CAPE
HENRY

French Ships of the Line under Mr de Barras

Water;ing Well

THE ATLANTIC

To the Delaware

G3834
.. V6 S3
1781
.T5
Fadm 90

This highly detailed map of Yorktown and the mouth of the Chesapeake Bay was
published in London shortly after the siege. It clearly shows the French fleet (blue circle)
guarding the entrance of the bay (blue arc). The town of York is on the left (red circle).

What was happening on the seas? Cornwallis was facing a series of disappointments, one after another.

In early September, Cornwallis received a distressing note from Clinton in New York. It read: "By intelligence which I have this day received, it would seem that Mr. Washington is moving an army to the southward with an appearance of haste, and . . . he expects the cooperation of a considerable French [military force]."

Then, Cornwallis received news of a naval battle: The French fleet had conquered the British, a rare victory for the French navy over the Royal Navy. Now he could only cling to the hope that an additional fleet was expected in New York from Britain and would manage to come to his aid. On September 17, he wrote to Clinton, "My provisions will last at least six weeks from this day." Then, Cornwallis learned that Admiral de Barras's fleet had arrived from Rhode Island. The French now had firm control over the Chesapeake Bay. He knew what this meant: He was surrounded. The land forces could now begin their work of slowly placing a wall of artillery around him. His next letter to Clinton read, "This place is in no state of defense. If you cannot relieve me very soon, you must be prepared to hear the worst."

As an experienced military officer, Cornwallis knew what was coming next. It would not be a battle in which two armies fought on a field and one claimed victory. This would be a classic European siege, a methodical process of encircling an enemy and gradually cutting him off from supply lines, using artillery to destroy his defenses, and squeezing ever more tightly until surrender was inevitable. It was a method used by both the British and the French. Only about twenty years earlier, in 1762, twelve thousand German and British troops had besieged five thousand French troops in Cassel (in present-day Germany). This time, the situation was

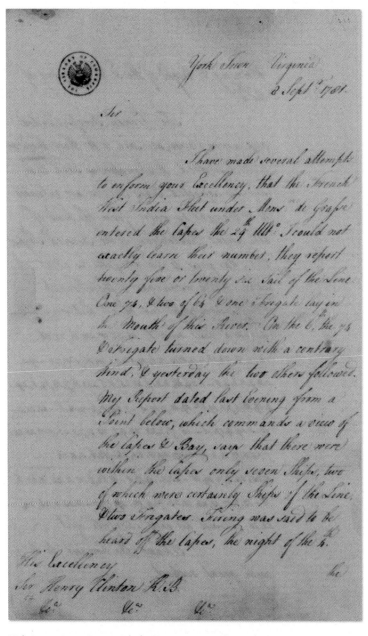

This letter from Cornwallis in Yorktown to Clinton in New York, dated September 8, 1781, informed Clinton that the French West India fleet under de Grasse had entered the Chesapeake Bay.

reversed: The British were on the receiving end. Cornwallis knew that Rochambeau would provide expert siege warfare guidance. The British general needed to mentally prepare his troops for what was to come: hunger, disease, boredom—and a concentrated artillery attack. He wasn't sure the Americans had the big guns, but the odds in a siege usually were on the side of the offense.

But Cornwallis was never one to lie down and accept a situation. Under severe pressure, he would use whatever tools he had to fight. He remained confident that reinforcements would arrive and that the Royal Navy would rescue him. Lafayette once described Cornwallis as "a bold and active man, two dangerous qualities in this Southern war." Indeed, the British general was not entirely out of options.

In the predawn hours of September 22, the tide and wind were moving down the York River. Three French warships lay at anchor at the river's mouth, monitoring traffic. At 2:00 A.M. in the quiet night, lookouts on the ships spotted an eerie and deadly sight. Out of the darkness, five unmanned vessels with sails ablaze, their helms tied together and their combustible cargoes set to blow, were headed right at them. Fireships! "In the dark night it was a beautiful and at the same time devastating sight," recalled French officer Karl Tornquist.

If the French ships couldn't get out of the way, the flames would torch them. The sailors furiously shouted directions to one another, trying to move away. Two of the targets avoided damage by slipping their anchors, but the *Triton* ran aground just as a fireship was getting closer. The crew frantically fired cannons at it, which successfully altered the ship's course. Tornquist noted, "It passed, however, so close to the square stern that no one could remain on the afterdeck."

What were the British hoping to achieve? Cause a distraction to delay the coming siege? Force de Grasse's ships back and open an escape passage? Could the British navy gain control of the river for one night, sneak troops out to open land, and march south? Unfortunately for the British, their timing was off, and the French ships managed to cut their anchors and escape.

De Grasse was not amused. Unaware that not all the allied troops had yet arrived, he was getting increasingly impatient. The following day, he dashed off a quick note to Washington: "It is time to begin to close in on the enemy, and to give him a taste of our combined strength." But patience was the key. It took time for all the pieces to come together, all the supplies to arrive from the North, the trenches dug, the artillery positioned. De Grasse may have felt like an idle spectator standing guard, though the presence of his navy was vital to the plan.

As long as the French navy held superior numbers, Cornwallis could not be reinforced or rescued. But on September 23, Washington received an urgent dispatch from the president of Congress warning him that Admiral Digby was almost at New York with ten additional British ships of the line. If the British were mounting a rescue mission, then time was of the essence. Washington became alarmed when de Grasse, upon hearing the message, threatened to withdraw his ships near Yorktown to the entrance of the bay. Washington sent a panicked letter to the admiral that read: "I cannot conceal from your Excellency the painful anxiety under which I have labored since the receipt of [your] letter . . . I must earnestly entreat your Excellency . . . to consider . . . that if you should withdraw your maritime force from the position agreed upon that no future day can restore to us a similar occasion for striking a decisive blow."

Militias were trickling in from around Virginia, and by September

26 all the Northern troops had finally arrived. The allied force now numbered around 19,000, including 3,000 American militiamen (mostly from Virginia). On top of that, almost 20,000 French sailors were stationed on the ships dotting the bay. This made a grand total of close to 40,000 allies ready to confront Cornwallis's army of 7,000 to 9,000 soldiers. For a short time, the combined allied camp would be the largest "city" in America.

On September 28, in oppressive heat, the allied troops marched the twelve miles from Williamsburg to the outskirts of Yorktown. The sun beat down, heating the sandy roadbed and burning the feet of those soldiers who were without shoes due to poor army finances. A French officer wrote of the heat, "I can testify to having suffered every affliction imaginable. We left nearly 800 soldiers in the rear. Two fell at my feet and died on the spot." Dense pine and cedar forest provided some shade and filled the air with pungent pine scent. Four miles outside Yorktown, the French veered left and the Americans turned right. They knew the enemy was watching and had expected to face some resistance from them. Why the quiet? The engineers stayed busy fixing the bridges that the British had destroyed along the way. The troops eventually stopped to build camp a mile from the outer British lines.

Washington and Rochambeau inspected the British position from afar, then sent reconnaissance teams forward to gather more intelligence. They set up their headquarters about a third of a mile apart, well beyond enemy artillery range and the main troop encampments. Washington traveled with two large white tents, one containing his sleeping and office quarters, the other his dining area. Following European procedure, the Americans laid out camp

This detail from a painting by Charles Willson Peale created in 1781 shows a Continental army encampment with tents increasing in size according to rank.

in order of battle: the noncommissioned officers and privates of a company first, with two feet between tents; junior grade officers next, followed by field commanders. Support services stood behind: paymaster, quartermaster, surgeons. Kitchens and sutlers (military store) were next, with horses and wagons far behind. Soldiers dug latrines three hundred feet away. Camp guards were stationed nine hundred feet in front of and behind the camp. Soon, the sound of drums filled the camp. The drumbeat dominated camp life and directed its functions. Drum cadences signaled reveille, assembly, to arms, retreat, and tattoo (lights-out).

Regarding camp life, two challenges faced the allied armies: a shortage of drinking water and a prevalence of disease. The British had intentionally spoiled clean water by tainting wells with the heads of steers, carcasses of horses, and other animals. To address disease, Washington forbade contact with outsiders. "The Commander in Chief forbids the officers or soldiers of the Army having any communication with the houses or inhabitants of the neighborhood or borrowing any utensils from them." Doctors checked all deserters from the British lines carefully for any signs of smallpox, and regular checks of American soldiers weeded out anyone with smallpox symptoms. Malarial fever, spread by mosquitoes, was another danger due to swampy land nearby.

Chapter

18

The Siege Begins

The British were watching. They had a long history of fighting the French, and those familiar white uniforms brought back memories for the military veterans. British officers knew their enemy, his style and techniques. The French were not to be trifled with, and a combined American and French force just might prove a challenge.

Cornwallis's troops had built a main line of defenses around Yorktown, connecting eight enclosed earthworks, called redoubts, with ten or so gun platforms for groups of cannons, called batteries. They had placed sixty-five cannons along the perimeter, the largest able to fire eighteen-pound cannonballs. A series of outer works stood farther from the town, as a first line of defense. These featured seven small earthworks. Three outlying redoubts guarded key land on the outside line. The most powerful of these, shaped like a star, was defended by 150 men of the elite Royal Welsh Fusiliers, who had been in the war since the very first battle at Lexington, Massachusetts. This redoubt sat high on a bluff north of town and watched river traffic. Two others, redoubts 9 and 10, guarded the southern approach to town.

On September 29, a British ship carrying a letter from New York slipped through the French blockade. Clinton promised that twenty-three ships of the line carrying five thousand soldiers would leave New York on October 5. This good news

The French army was known for its white uniforms, with different-colored collars, cuffs, and sometimes vests to indicate the individual's regiment.

buoyed Cornwallis's spirits and gave him renewed hope. He replied to Clinton: "Your letter . . . has given me the greatest satisfaction. I shall retire this night within the [earth]works, and have no doubt, if relief arrives in any reasonable time, York[town] and Gloucester will be both in possession of his Majesty's troops."

Cornwallis just needed to hold firm. However, he was surrounded and his troops spread thin. A concentrated effort by the allies could break through his lines. After consulting with his officers, he decided to withdraw from most of his outer defenses and concentrate his power in the remaining defenses, in hopes the allies' artillery would not start their attack until close to the arrival of his reinforcements.

When they noticed no activity in the enemy's outer defenses, a few French soldiers cautiously crept forward to find out why. To their surprise, they found them empty. They sent word immediately to Rochambeau. He was stunned. Why would Cornwallis withdraw already? He and Washington puzzled over what it meant. Whatever Cornwallis's reason, the move was to the allies' benefit and would save them time and effort in the long run—they simply had to move forward and not have to take the outer defenses by force. However, three redoubts—9, 10, and the Fusiliers'—all remained secured by the British.

As engineers worked to shore up the abandoned defenses and modify them for the American and French forces, the British side stayed mostly silent; they refrained from firing on the allies, to the puzzlement of the officers. "I am at a loss to account

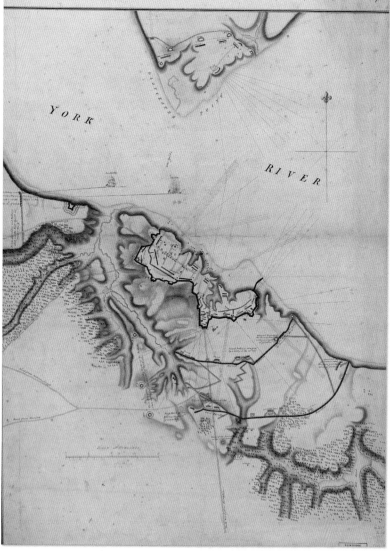

PLAN of YORK TOWN and GLOUCESTER in VIRGINIA Shewing the WORKS constructed for the Defence of those POSTS by the R.Hon.ble Lieut.General EARL CORNWALLIS with the Attacks of the Combined ARMY of FRENCH and REBELS under the Command of the Generals Count de ROCHAMBAUD and WASHINGTON which Capitulated October 1781

This military map of Yorktown and Gloucester details the British defenses (in red) and shows the eventual allied siege lines (in blue).

for it, for the moon shone bright, and by the help of their night glasses they must certainly have discovered us," wrote Captain James Duncan. The next day, the British artillery did open fire to disrupt progress on the fortifications. General Thomas Nelson Jr. wrote, "The enemy endeavored to retard these operations by playing on our men who were at work . . . We have not returned one shot."

On October 1, Washington approved the final plan for the siege as proposed by French engineers. The French had invented much of the standard siege procedure, roughly one hundred years earlier. Soldiers dug rings of earthworks and erected gun batteries progressively closer to the enemy. They first dug a trench, called the first parallel or first siege line, six hundred yards from the enemy fortifications, beyond the range of small arms. Soldiers called miners and sappers, who were experienced with digging, and many with mining backgrounds, would do their work at night, trying not to attract British attention. They would dig a three-foot-deep trench and pile the dirt three feet high on the side toward the enemy to create a safe passageway. They used some dirt to create foundations for gun platforms. The finished siege line looked like a big necklace strung with redoubts and gun batteries. When the siege line was ready and the big guns in place, the artillery would begin pounding the enemy. Only Washington, Rochambeau, and a few high-ranking officers knew all the details for the siege. Secrecy was vital.

Much construction work on gun platforms and the trenches would need to be completed before the siege could begin. Work continued for a week. Some troops guarded the builders, while others carried out reconnaissance, scouting locations for

This scene depicts General Washington (second from left) and five of his generals at Yorktown. Lafayette is on the left; Rochambeau is in red. The windmill was a landmark of Yorktown. Note the sunken ships and the dead horses on the beach, seeming to indicate the siege is over.

constructing the first siege parallel (trench). Washington himself joined the scouting parties, under guard, and came as close as three hundred yards from enemy lines.

Washington had never participated in a siege before; Yorktown was the only siege conducted by the Continental Army during the entire war. Fortunately, the French army included some well-trained military engineers. And according to Baron von Closen, Rochambeau had participated in fourteen sieges during his career thus far. With his knowledge of siege warfare and Washington's familiarity with the landscape, they were a good team. But for the most part, Washington needed to trust the French and to sit back and be patient.

When the preparation stage was complete, it was time to start the dangerous job of digging the trenches that connected the gun platforms and allowed for protected movement of soldiers. The weather was cloudy and rainy. In the darkness, the sappers and miners, under the protection of three regiments, began digging. The army quartermasters had brought along five hundred spades, one hundred pickaxes, and four hundred axes and hatchets. Private Joseph Plumb Martin, a young soldier from western Massachusetts, was one of the miners and sappers. He later described an encounter in the trenches that he would never forget: "We had not proceeded far . . . before the engineers ordered us to [stop] and remain where we were . . . In a few minutes after their departure there came a man alone to us . . . and inquired for the engineers." The stranger asked which unit they were and chatted with them for a few minutes, then went off to find the engineers, "after strictly charging us, in case we should be taken prisoners, not to [tell] the enemy what troops we were. We were obliged to him for his kind advice, but we considered ourselves as standing in no great need of it . . . in a short time the engineers returned and the aforementioned stranger with them. They discoursed together some time, when by the officers often calling him 'Your Excellency,' we discovered that it was George Washington."

At a different location, another crew dug in darkness. General Washington appeared, grabbed a pickax, took a swing, and drove it into the dirt. It was a purely ceremonial action, but it showed his solidarity with his men. It was backbreaking work. The men commenced digging in silence, a steady patter of rain muffling the sounds of axes and shovels breaking into the Virginia earth. Could they keep this activity secret from the enemy? It hardly seemed possible. Fifteen hundred men were frantically digging a trench ten feet wide by three feet deep only six hundred yards from the British defenses. "The soil was light and sandy, and we worked like beavers all through the night," recalled Asa Redington from New Hampshire. One group of guards built large bonfires away from the work to distract the British gunners. By dawn, they had completed a half mile of trench. Washington was gleeful, and he wrote in his diary, "The work was executed with so much secrecy and dispatch that the enemy were, I believe, totally ignorant of our labor till the light of the morning discovered it to them."

The American gunners stayed silent. Washington and Rochambeau wanted to be sure that everything was in place before the siege began. All the big guns had to be positioned just right. When all the trenches and batteries were complete, they would open fire with a whole line of guns. If they had fired as each battery was complete, the British would have concentrated on that battery and blown it to bits.

Map of

SIEGE OF YORKTOWN

On September 28, 1781, the allied armies marched from Williamsburg to Yorktown to begin preparations for the siege. With the French navy in control of the Chesapeake Bay, the British were surrounded. For nine days—from October 9, when the first big French gun fired, to October 17, when the British surrendered—guns pounded the town of York.

MAP KEY

≡ ≡ ≡ ≡ Second Parallel	0 .5
– – – – First Parallel	MILES
⛵ British Ships	

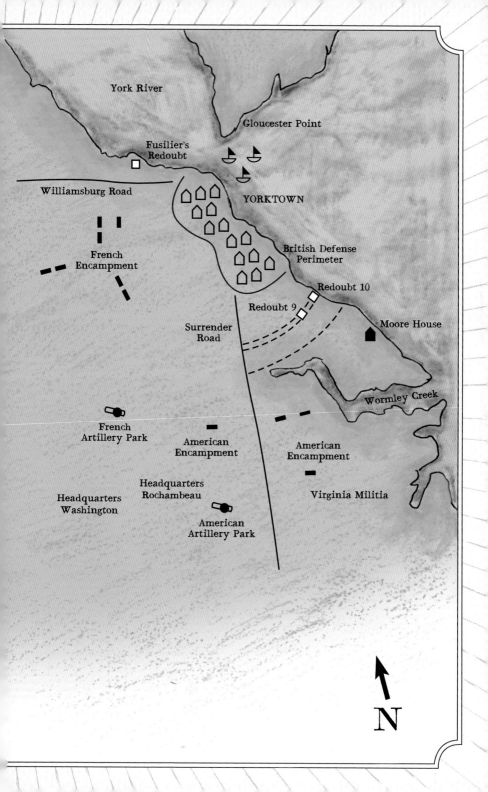

York River

Gloucester Point

Fusilier's
Redoubt

Williamsburg Road

YORKTOWN

French
Encampment

British Defense
Perimeter

Redoubt 10

Redoubt 9

Surrender
Road

Moore House

Wormley Creek

French
Artillery Park

American
Encampment

American
Encampment

Headquarters
Rochambeau

Headquarters
Washington

Virginia Militia

American
Artillery Park

N

On October 9, the first siege line was complete. Martin wrote, "All were upon the tiptoe of expectation and impatience to see the signal given to open the whole line of batteries." General Anthony Wayne expressed the allies' mood well when he wrote, "Everything is in readiness to commence the siege, our army is numerous and in high spirits, the French are the finest body of troops I ever viewed, and harmony and friendship pervades the whole."

At approximately 2:00 P.M., the French held a brief ceremony that traditionally opened a siege. Troops slowly raised flags above the trenches to mark their readiness for battle. The French band struck up a tune, and the white fleur-de-lis flag rose above the French batteries. The French troops cheered, "Huzzah for the Americans!" Washington, as overall commander, gave General Saint-Simon the honor of firing the first shot from the French trench. A twenty-four-pound cannonball soared through the air, scoring a direct hit on the enemy fortifications. By 5:00 P.M., the American guns were ready. Brigadier General Henry Knox, commander of the American artillery, was supposed to light the first ceremonial shot for the Americans, but he offered it to General Washington, who ignited the fuse and stood back. The eighteen-pound ball thundered from the cannon and flew through the air at a target in Yorktown. Colonel Philip Van Cortlandt of the Second New York Regiment recalled, "I could hear the ball strike from house to house and I was afterward informed that it went through the one where many of the officers were at dinner, and over the tables, [shattering] the dishes, and either killed or wounded the one at the head of the table."

The siege had officially begun. "This day, this happy day, we returned their fire," wrote a Pennsylvania soldier, expressing the common relief around camp that after so many days of tense preparation, the beginning of the end was underway. An American officer wrote, "Happy day! Forty-one mouths of fire [cannons] were suddenly unmasked."

A FEROCIOUS POUNDING

The siege would be the ultimate test for the American artillery. They could learn much from the French, considered experts.

The French had shipped twenty-eight siege guns, which fired eighteen- and twenty-four-pound balls, from France to Newport and from there to Jamestown, Virginia, then hauled them overland to Yorktown by oxen carts. This was no easy task, as each gun weighed up to six thousand pounds (more than an average hippopotamus). They were vital to the success of the campaign. Cornwallis had not anticipated the French heavy artillery. The total combined allied line of artillery included an estimated seventy-three pieces (it's impossible to know exact numbers, as sources vary greatly). The French and American defenses featured three types of artillery: cannons, mortars, and howitzers. Their sizes varied, and some of the mobile field cannons could be easily moved, while the siege guns could not. Some could fire solid shot (cannonballs) that could destroy earthworks and buildings; others fired grapeshot (a collection of small balls delivered at the same time) that spread out and damaged a wider area. Mortars shot shells that would explode in the air like a bomb and rain down shrapnel. A howitzer was capable of firing both balls and shells.

A crew of eight or nine men was required to fire the big guns. They men were aiming first for British cannons and large guns. A Pennsylvanian wrote that "shot and shells flew incessantly through the night, dismounted the guns of the enemy." It was a

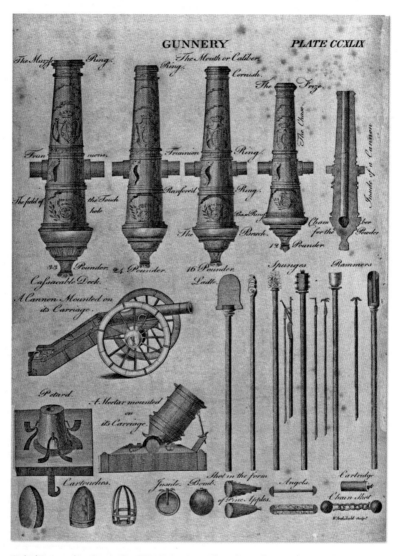

This illustration from the 1771 *Encyclopedia Britannica* shows a variety of cannon sizes used by the British military. The rammers pushed the ball into the cannon, and the sponges cleaned out the barrel for the next shot.

sight unlike any most of the Americans had ever witnessed before. An officer wrote that "a number of shells from the works of both parties passing high in the air, and descending in a curve, each with a long train of fire, exhibited a brilliant spectacle."

The following day, October 10, the shelling increased in intensity. Dr. James Thacher later described the scene: "[The bombs] are clearly visible in the form of a black ball in the day, but in the night, they appear like fiery meteors with blazing tails, most beautifully brilliant, ascending majestically from the mortar to a certain altitude, and gradually descending to the spot where they are destined to execute their work of destruction." A Frenchman named Claude Robin wrote of each bomb "sometimes burying itself in the roofs of houses, sometimes when it burst, raising clouds of dust and rubbish from the ruins of the buildings, at other times blowing the unfortunate wretches that happened to be within its reach, more than twenty feet high in the air, and letting them fall at a considerable distance most pitiably torn. Such terrible sights as these fix and captivate the attention, and fill the mind at the same instant with trouble, wonder, and consternation."

The ferocity of the guns created an earsplitting pounding that could be heard many miles away. A British officer later wrote that on the 10th, the fire from the allies was so intense that the British could scarcely fire their guns.

☆ ☆ ☆

When the bombs began to rain down on Yorktown, those few citizens who had refused to leave immediately knew they had made an error in judgment. As cannonballs smashed into his solid-stone house, sixty-five-year-old "Secretary" Thomas Nelson, the uncle

of the current Virginia governor, reconsidered his decision. Two of his sons serving in the American army asked Washington to allow Nelson to evacuate Yorktown. Cornwallis approved Washington's request for a temporary cease-fire, and at noon on October 10, Nelson left Yorktown under a flag of truce. The gout-afflicted older man was taken to Washington's headquarters, along with his slave (who had managed to smuggle out the family silver hidden in a pile of blankets). Nelson was able to provide valuable firsthand evidence of the bombardment's effect on the town.

St. George Tucker, a major in the Virginia militia, dined with him the following day and reported that Nelson told him there had been a direct hit on the house in the opening bombardment, with two British officers killed and one wounded by a bomb. Nelson also related that the citizens of Yorktown were massing at the river's edge, trying to escape the destruction by finding refuge

This watercolor by an unknown artist, most likely a British soldier, shows Yorktown during the siege from across the river in Gloucester.

in the base of the steep cliffs there. Cornwallis, too, had moved down to the river, reportedly taking shelter in a cave dug into the cliffs. Nelson also stated that a British major, Charles Cochrane, had arrived from New York.

After a seven-day trip, Cochrane's whaleboat, its twelve oars muffled, had silently slipped by the French patrols. He carried an urgent message from Clinton: "I am doing everything in my power to relieve you by a direct move, and I have reason to hope, from the assurances given me this day by Admiral Graves, that we may pass the [sand]bar by the 12th of Oct." Graves was planning to leave for Yorktown with thirty ships of the line to attack de Grasse and bring reinforcements. Cornwallis replied, "Nothing but a direct move to York River which includes a successful naval action can save us . . . We cannot hope to make a very long resistance."

The courier, Major Cochrane, perhaps eager to have a story to tell from the battlefield, asked to fire a gun. A captain later described what happened: "anxious to see its effect, [Cochrane] looked over [the wall] to observe it, when his head was carried off by a cannon ball."

Washington was elated when he heard that the Royal Navy had been delayed again. Time was running out for Cornwallis. Washington dared to write what he hoped would be the outcome: "We anticipate the reduction of Lord Cornwallis with his army, with much satisfaction."

The allies were continually looking for clues to the conditions behind enemy lines. British deserters had estimated that two thousand of Cornwallis's soldiers were ill in the hospital. They said that food supplies were dwindling and forage for the livestock was scarce. American officers looked through spyglasses and observed dead horses floating in the river and lying onshore. They counted seventy to a hundred one day, nearly four hundred the next, and guessed that the British had been forced to shoot them due to lack of feed. The big question on everyone's mind was, How long could Cornwallis hold out? But the allied leaders all knew that if anyone could find a way out of a mess, it was Cornwallis.

Washington constantly worried that Cornwallis would find a way to escape that he hadn't anticipated. As the Americans saw it, Cornwallis had only two ways to flee: fight up the peninsula if reinforcements managed to arrive (this required a sea battle with de Grasse) or, much less likely, cross the York River to Gloucester and make a run for it. Washington had directed Lauzun's Legion, under the duc de Lauzun, to a position at Gloucester Point. The legion was a foreign corps with men from at least fifteen European countries. The combined cavalry, artillery, and infantry troops were supported by fifteen hundred Virginia militiamen.

One way to prevent Cornwallis from fleeing by water was to destroy his remaining ships. It was time for a dangerous weapon: hot shot. The French had constructed an oven for heating cannonballs. The shot was heated red hot, until it glowed. The gunners packed the cannon barrel with powder and then with dirt or damp hay to insulate it and prevent the powder from igniting accidentally when they rammed the red-hot ball into the barrel. In the risky procedure, gunners used special tongs brought from France to handle the balls. Well-aimed hot shot set wooden ships or other structures ablaze and could destroy an entire ship if it hit the powder supply.

At 8:00 P.M. on October 10, the French artillery began firing hot shot at the two large British ships: the twenty-six-gun frigate *Guadaloupe*, which had taken refuge in the Yorktown harbor in the shadow of the cliffs, and the forty-four-gun flagship *Charon* (which had carried Benedict Arnold to Virginia). The resulting show impressed numerous witnesses who described it. The *Charon* received a direct hit and, while attempting to flee, collided with a transport. Dr. Thacher wrote, "The ships were enwrapped in a torrent of fire, spreading with vivid brightness among the combustible rigging, and running with amazing rapidity to the tops of several masts, while all around was thunder and lightning from our numerous cannon and mortars . . . one of the most sublime and magnificent spectacles which can be imagined. Some of our shells overreaching the town, are seen to fall into the river, and bursting, throw up columns of water like the spouting of the monsters of the deep." A senior French officer wrote, "Never could a more horrible or more beautiful spectacle be seen. On a dark

A modern illustration showing what the French artillery park at Yorktown most likely looked like. An artillery park was where the artillery and its various accessories, like carriages for transporting it and ammunition, were gathered in one place.

night, the ships with all their open portholes discharging sheafs of fire, the cannon shots that were going off, the appearance of the whole [harbor], the ships under topsails flying from the burning vessels, all that formed a terrible and sublime spectacle."

Blazing balls flying through the red sky proved such an attraction that citizens of Yorktown risked their safety to climb to high places to watch. One witness wrote later, "I never saw anything so magnificent."

Morning light revealed a smoldering harbor of burned-out ships. Cornwallis was stunned. The *Charon* was a charred heap; two other transports were barely noticeable above the water. Only the *Guadaloupe*, anchored by the bluff, remained.

Artillery boomed continuously through the day. The noise was deafening. Load! Ram! Fire! Chargez! Bourrez! Feu! The best gun crews could fire five times per hour.

British crews could barely fire their guns due to the incessant explosions. "The heavy fire forced us to throw our tents into the ditches . . . We could find no refuge in or out of town . . . many were killed by bursting bombs . . . the greater part of the town lies in ashes, and two batteries have been completely dismantled," wrote a Hessian private named Stephan Popp in his diary.

"The entire night was an immense roar of bursting shell," wrote Captain Duncan. On the British side, Lieutenant Bartholomew James from the *Charon* estimated that upwards of a thousand shells were fired at Yorktown overnight.

A Hessian, Johann Döhla, had never seen such an intense bombardment and guessed he never would again.

I saw bombs fall into the water and lie there
for five, six, eight and more minutes and then

still explode . . . It showered upon the river
bank the sand and mud from below; if one sat
there, it felt like the shocks of an earthquake.
The fragments and pieces of these bombs flew
back again and fell on the houses and buildings
of the city and in our camp, where they still
did much damage and robbed many a brave
soldier of his life or struck off his arm and leg.
I had myself a piece of an exploded bomb in
my hands which weighed more than 30 pounds
and was over three inches thick.

At dusk the next day, the Americans and French moved forward with their shovels, axes, and hoes to begin digging a second siege line even closer to the enemy. Lieutenant William Felt-
man of Pennsylvania wrote that within an hour, they had gone
deep enough to provide cover from the British fire. Washington
thought the British the next morning were just as surprised this
time around: "By their conduct and mode of firing, [the British
did not] appear to have had any suspicion of our working parties
till day light [revealed] them."

Next, it was time for the officers to begin strategizing how to capture redoubts 9 and 10, the last British barriers to completing the
second parallel. Redoubts 9 and 10 lay on the southeast approach
to Yorktown, outside the main perimeter line, where the land was
flat and less easy to defend. Redoubt 9 was pentagon-shaped, the
larger of the two. Redoubt 10 was square-shaped and close to the
river bluff, guarded by seventy British and Hessian soldiers. Americans called it the "Rock Redoubt."

CHAPTER

20

STORMING THE REDOUBTS

Rochambeau was not sufficiently convinced that the British redoubts had been pounded enough to make them easy to conquer. He and his son Donatien did some stealth reconnaissance to see if the last two remaining redoubts were ready for attack. Rochambeau ordered more cannon fire, and on October 13 he wrote, "Nou verrons demain si la poire est mûre." (We shall see tomorrow if the pear is ripe.) The two armies were working well together. Adjutant General Edward Hand observed, "Never did greater harmony subsist between two armies than between the French and Americans. Their only [contention] is who shall do most."

Up to this point, the artillery had done the bulk of the work, but now it was the infantry's turn. Capturing the redoubts was necessary for the last step of the siege. There would be simultaneous attacks, with the French storming redoubt 9 and the Americans, redoubt 10. The miners and sappers were sent out one last time to clear debris from the attack route.

To capture a redoubt, soldiers needed to conquer a number of obstacles. A redoubt was enclosed by a high mound of earth called a parapet. In front of the parapet was a moat or ditch up to seven feet deep. Three more obstacles ensured that attackers would face a tough challenge. First, there was a wall of abatis, large tree branches, some sharpened to a point, with their trunks partially buried in the ground. Next were fraises, long logs with pointed ends that were placed at an angle near the base of the parapet and extended out over the ditch. Finally, palisades, vertical logs pointed at the ends, were driven into the bottom of the ditch.

The following day, the troops completed the second parallel trench. It was time to storm the redoubts. But who would lead the charges? The French chose Guillaume, comte de Deux-Ponts. For the Americans, Lafayette chose his aide and favorite staff officer, a Frenchman, Lieutenant Colonel Jean de Gimat. Colonel Alexander Hamilton was not pleased. He was Officer of the Day and felt he should have the honor. For four years, he had longed for battlefield glory but had been stuck with a desk job as an aide to General Washington. Washington kept spurning his requests to lead a battalion. Hamilton expressed interest in foreign posts as well but never got approved for those.

The previous February, Hamilton's frustration had gotten the best of him. In a sharp exchange of words, the general had reprimanded his aide for making him wait for a meeting. He had accused Hamilton of treating him with disrespect. Hamilton took offense and quit his job on the spot. Washington later reached out to Hamilton with an apology, but the damage had been done. Hamilton followed through and left Washington's staff. Despite the tiff, Washington had remained loyal to Hamilton. Finally, in late July, he had assigned Hamilton command of a New York infantry battalion. Hamilton had marched down to Virginia with his troops and was on the battlefield at Yorktown, still hoping to prove his leadership abilities.

Hamilton and Lafayette had both served as aides to Washington and were friends. But this was too much. Lafayette was robbing him of what could be a last great chance to fight. Hamilton fired off a note to Washington pleading for the right to lead the attack. "We have it! We have it!" he shouted when Washington

Alexander Hamilton as a Soldier portrays Hamilton at Yorktown and was painted by Alonzo Chappel in 1857.

consented. Hamilton would command three battalions made up of men from Massachusetts, Connecticut, New Hampshire, and Rhode Island. This most likely included the First Rhode Island Regiment: 197 black light infantrymen led by white officers. (Historians don't all agree that they participated.) They were known throughout the army and had successfully beaten back assaults by Hessian troops at the Battle of Rhode Island in August 1778.

One battalion was commanded by Lafayette's friend John Laurens from South Carolina, the former aide to Washington who had advocated for the army's recruitment of slaves. Most recently, he had been assigned to a diplomatic mission in France; only months before, he had stood in the French king's court representing the United States. His column was tasked with stopping any enemy retreat.

As darkness grew, the French and American guns gradually fell silent. Could the British predict what was coming? Hamilton assembled his troops, and General Washington gave them a pep talk, inspiring them to be brave.

Joseph Plumb Martin described the process: "The Sappers and Miners were furnished with axes and were to proceed in front and cut a passage for the troops through the abatis . . . It is almost impossible to get through them. Through these we were to cut a passage before we or the other assailants could enter."

At dark, the men advanced beyond the trench and lay on the ground, awaiting the signal to proceed. The watchword was "Rochambeau," a good rallying cry, for *Ro-sham-bow*, when pronounced quickly, sounded like *Rush-on-boys*.

In Martin's words: "We had not lain here long before the expected signal was given, for us and the French, who were to storm the other redoubt . . . three shells with their fiery trains mounting the air in quick succession. The word *up, up,* was then reiterated through the detachment. We immediately moved silently on toward the redoubt . . . with unloaded muskets." Washington and Lafayette had ordered only bayonets, to ensure that no musket was discharged early to spoil the element of surprise.

The French and Americans moved forward simultaneously. Martin's sappers began cutting through the abatis. Hamilton's four hundred men moved quietly, but the British suddenly spotted the movement and let loose a round of grapeshot shells and cannonballs. The Americans lost patience and charged with a loud "Huzzah!" The artillery had done its job over the previous days, and large holes in the defense work allowed entrance. They clawed through the abatis, scrambled into the ditch, climbed over the palisades, clambered between the fraises, and ascended the parapets, stunning the seventy British and German soldiers inside. Surprised and overwhelmed, the defenders barely put up a fight, and many surrendered. After ten minutes of hand-to-hand combat, the redoubt belonged to the Americans. Hamilton was ecstatic! The cost had been nine dead and twenty-five wounded. Hamilton's moment of battlefield glory was complete.

Standing upon redoubt 10, Lafayette sent a quick note to the comte de Deux-Ponts informing him the Americans had been successful. Where was he? A note returned saying the French were not quite victorious . . . yet. Earlier in the day, the French commanders had suggested that, given French expertise, their troops should attack both redoubts. Lafayette immediately quashed that idea, offended at the suggestion since he was an officer in the American army. Redoubt 9 had received less artillery damage, so it was stronger, and the French had encountered more resistance. Unlike the Americans, the French soldiers carried loaded

This painting depicts the Americans storming redoubt 10. It was painted about sixty years after the event.

weapons. With the shout "Vive le roi!" (Long live the king!), they charged ahead, firing at the 125 enemy soldiers. In thirty minutes, though with greater casualties, the French were victorious.

With the two British redoubts captured, the allies were now just outside Yorktown. They quickly moved cannons into the redoubts and secured the gun platforms, working throughout the night to complete the second siege line. It stretched almost three-quarters of a mile. Early the next morning, General Washington offered praise: "the Commander in Chief congratulates the Allied Army on the success of the enterprise last evening against the two important works on the left of the enemy's line."

In the early morning hours of October 16, some 350 British soldiers silently moved out of the defenses and crossed the field between the two armies. They were on a mission of desperation, planning to cripple the unfinished work of the allies. If successful, it could perhaps buy some time. There was still hope that the British navy might somehow miraculously appear. They caught the French completely by surprise and killed a number of them. They also managed to "spike" several cannons, the act of sticking bayonets into the vent holes and snapping them off, thus temporarily rendering them useless. They were quickly chased out, however, and order was restored. Cornwallis later wrote, "This action, though extremely honorable to the officers and soldiers who executed it, proved of little public advantage . . . for the cannon having been spiked in a hurry, were soon rendered fit for service again, and before dark the whole parallel and batteries appeared to be nearly complete." To the allies, it demonstrated how desperate the British had become.

As guns continued to pound Yorktown, Cornwallis assessed his grim situation. He was running low on ammunition and food, his troops were sick, morale was low, and disease was threatening to bring more devastation. The constant barrage was driving the men out of their minds and giving them little time to return fire.

With a dwindling food supply, Cornwallis had to find a way to stretch the provisions until the navy arrived. He ordered all but two thousand of the slaves taking refuge in Yorktown expelled from British lines. Many were very ill with smallpox and other illnesses. Terrified of returning to their owners, they took shelter in the woods around Yorktown and foraged for whatever food they could find. Hundreds lay down in the no-man's-land between the armies and starved to death or died of exposure and disease. They had come to the British for protection and freedom. The refuge the British had promised turned into utter cruelty in the face of self-preservation.

By this point, Cornwallis knew the navy was not coming in time to rescue him. But never one to give up, he devised a plan that just might work—and the only option he had left. Escape! He had managed to locate sixteen large boats. He would transport his able-bodied troops across the York River to Gloucester Point. He calculated that it would take three trips. Once they landed, the British artillery would need to blast an exit hole through Lauzun's defenses that were surrounding the peninsula. His troops would then rush through and either escape to the north and head for New York or head south to Charles Town. At around 10:00 P.M. on October 16, he put the plan into action, and the first wave of boats headed for Gloucester. In the darkness, if they kept quiet, they might have a chance.

But the weather did not cooperate. A huge storm struck, and

the choppy river threatened to capsize the boats. Hessian officer Johann von Ewald wrote, "It was as dark as a sack and one could neither see nor hear anything because of the awful downpour and heavy gale . . . there was the most severe thunderstorm, but the violent flashes of lightning benefited us, since we could at least see around us for an instant." Some boats reached the opposite shore, while a few blew downstream, but these were all captured by the allied troops. By 2:00 A.M., the storm had blown through, but the boats were scattered, some even sunk. By now, the allies were aware of the attempt, and the plan had to be aborted. Banastre Tarleton concluded, "Thus expired the last hope of the British army."

CHAPTER

21

A DEAFENING QUIET

By now, more than seventy cannons and mortars had been in continual operation for more than twenty-four hours. Someone counted thirty-six hundred shots within a twenty-four-hour period. Dr. James Thacher summed it up: "The whole peninsula trembles under the incessant thunderings of our infernal machines. We have leveled some of their works in ruins and silenced their guns; they have almost ceased firing. We are so near as to have a distinct view of the dreadful havoc and destruction . . . the scene is drawing to a close."

At 10:00 A.M. on October 17, a lone British drummer boy appeared on a parapet and began to beat the signal to request parley (a meeting of opposing sides). Beside him stood an officer waving a white handkerchief. No one could hear the drum above the pounding guns, but the white handkerchief spoke volumes. There was a ripple of silence as gunners all along the lines stopped firing. The lone drum pounded out its message. "I thought I never heard a drum equal to it—the most delightful music to us all," twenty-year-old Lieutenant Ebenezer Denny of Pennsylvania wrote in his journal.

Earlier that morning, Cornwallis had met with his top officers. They knew their defenses were crumbling fast and wouldn't hold. Cornwallis decided it would be "wanton and inhuman to the last degree to sacrifice the lives of this small body of gallant soldiers who had ever behaved with so much fidelity and courage, by exposing them to an assault which from numbers and precautions of the enemy could not fail to succeed."

An American soldier walked to the British messenger, tied a blindfold around his eyes, and led him into the allied defenses. An unearthly quiet settled over the battlefield. There were no birds left to chirp.

At his headquarters, George Washington may have wondered why the guns had stopped. An aide handed him a note. Washington broke the seal and read:

> Sir, I propose a cessation of hostilities for twenty-four hours, and that two officers be appointed from each side, to meet at Mr. Moore's house, to settle terms for the surrender of the posts at York and Gloucester. I have the honour to be, &c Cornwallis

It was the moment the allies had been dreaming of for months. Coincidentally, it was four years to the day since the last British surrender, at Saratoga, the action that had enticed France to join the war.

In the quiet, thousands now waited for the process of negotiation. General Washington had decisions to make. The British messenger returned to his camp with a response, and many messages traveled between the camps in the following hours. The day wound down, and both sides wondered what tomorrow would bring. Major St. George Tucker wrote his wife: "A solemn stillness prevailed. The night was remarkably clear, and the sky decorated with ten thousand stars. Numberless meteors gleaming through the atmosphere afforded a pleasing resemblance to the bombs which had exhibited a noble firework the night before, but happily divested of all their horror."

At dawn, the allied troops heard the unmistakable wheeze of bagpipes coming from the British lines, a Scottish serenade. A French band returned a tune.

"As soon as the sun rose, one of the most striking pictures of war was displayed that imagination can paint . . . their parapets crowded with officers looking at those who were assembled at the top of our works," St. George Tucker wrote from the American side.

Throughout the rest of the day, couriers carried many more messages between the sides. Cornwallis proposed that four nego-tiators, two British and two from the allies, meet at the house of Augustine Moore, which sat on the York River outside the line of fire, convenient to both sides and a mile from the destruction of Yorktown. Washington and Rochambeau selected Colonel John Laurens (who had been present at the last American surrender, in Charles Town) and Louis-Marie, vicomte de Noailles, Lafayette's brother-in-law. When the negotiators met at the Moore house, one of the sticking points was that the Americans wanted to deny the British army "full honors of war," since the British had done the same to the Americans at Charles Town. Honors of war were a set of privileges granted to a defeated army that included flags fly-ing, bayonets fixed (attached), and a band playing. They typically applied to a sovereign or independent nation, and technically the Americans weren't really a sovereign nation in Britain's eyes. Now the British saw the Americans as vindictive.

The negotiations continued into the night. When Washing-ton and Rochambeau agreed to a final version, they sent it to Cornwallis. Around 11:00 A.M. the following day, October 19, Cornwallis dipped his pen into ink and scribbled his signature, making it official. When Washington and Rochambeau signed it, the Siege of Yorktown was over.

American and French troops moved into the British fortifications.

The enemy lowered the British flag and evacuated, moving their camps to the beach area under the cliffs. The Royal Welsh Fusiliers abandoned their redoubt on the river bluff, which the allies had not captured. Cornwallis issued a note of thanks to his troops: "Lord Cornwallis cannot express enough the gratitude due the officers and soldiers of this army for their good [performance] on every occasion while he had the honor to command them." He praised their extraordinary courage and resolution, and added, "The blood of the noblest man will not have been in vain."

The sun shone brightly that afternoon, a crisp fall day, the trees showing the first tinges of autumnal color. Word had spread fast, and civilians from far and wide arrived in carriages and wagons, and on horseback, to witness the surrender of the mighty British forces. The American and French troops lined up in two rows facing each other, stretching more than a mile along the Hampton Road. The French wore pressed white uniforms with colored lapels and waistcoats representing different regiments and black three-cornered cocked hats. The Americans wore an assortment of uniforms, from shabby Continental blue to the leather hunting shirts of the militia.

Tunes from a French military band, the only band in the allied forces, wafted over the meadow.

Washington, Rochambeau, Lafayette, and other senior officers rode out to the meeting point. The American general sat, back erect, atop his favorite horse, Nelson, given to him by General Thomas Nelson. The chestnut-colored horse with a white

Articles of Capitulation settled between his
Excellency General Washington Comander in
Chief of the combined Forces of America & France
— his Excellency the Count de Rochambeau
Lieutenant General of the Armies of the King
of France — Great Cross of the Royal & Military
Order of St. Louis — Commanding the Auxiliary
Troops of his most Christian Majesty in Ame=
=rica. — And his Excellency the Count de
Grasse Lieutenant General of the Naval Armies
of his most Christian Majesty, Commander of
the Order of St. Louis, comand'g in Chief the Na
val Army of France in the Chesapeak — on
the one Part — And his Excellency the
Right Hon.ble Earl Cornwallis Lieut General
of his Britannick Majesty's Forces, commanding
the Garrisons of York & Gloucester and Thomas
Symonds Esq. Commanding his Britannick
Majesty's Naval forces in York river in Virginia
on the other part.

Article 1st

The Articles of Capitulation laid out the terms of the surrender and were the result of negotiation and compromise.

This iconic and huge (12' x18') painting of the surrender at Yorktown is located high up in the dome of the United States Capitol building in Washington, DC. Congress commissioned the American artist John Trumbull to paint a series of scenes from American history. The central figures are British General Charles O'Hara and American General Benjamin Lincoln.

blaze on his face had most likely been born near Yorktown, General Nelson's home.

Former Washington aides, now commanders, John Laurens and Alexander Hamilton stood with their men, waiting.

At about 3:00 P.M., an hour later than scheduled, the assembled crowd heard the faint sounds of fifes and drums coming from the direction of Yorktown. A parade of four thousand redcoats in clean uniforms marched with slow and solemn steps between the allies. Their flags were cased (wrapped in black material) per the agreement, and their fifes played a melancholy British air. Fully half of the British troops lay back in Yorktown, sick or wounded.

Lafayette stood watching the ceremony. No record of his feelings at the sight exists, but no doubt he, like all the others, felt extreme satisfaction. After his months of shadowing Cornwallis, the anxiety and hard work were at an end. His countrymen had come through at the right time. And the great leader, his mentor, General George Washington, had sacrificed so much to bring the army to this point.

As the front of the procession came near the allied leaders, they realized someone was missing. Where was Cornwallis? Washington and Rochambeau wondered. "Every eye was prepared to gaze on Lord Cornwallis . . . but he disappointed our expectations," wrote Dr. Thacher. Instead, Brigadier General Charles O'Hara led the procession. At the delegation of leaders, he veered left and approached Rochambeau's adjutant, asking for the French general. The adjutant quickly realized that O'Hara was planning to surrender Cornwallis's sword to Rochambeau and moved between them to steer him toward Washington, saying, "You are mistaken, the commander-in-chief of our army is on the

Normally, the musicians of the losing side played a tune of the victor during surrender. The articles of this surrender, however, required the British to play a British or German tune. While it has been widely repeated that the tune's title was "The World Turned Upside Down," a popular tune of the period, historians can find no direct evidence from the time stating definitely that this was the tune.

right." Was O'Hara trying to slight Washington? He explained that Lord Cornwallis was ill. Ill or too embarrassed, wondered Dr. Thacher in his journal, writing, "We are not to be surprised that the pride of the British officer is humbled on this occasion." O'Hara offered Cornwallis's sword to Washington, who declined to receive it. He referred Cornwallis's second-in-command to his own second-in-command, Benjamin Lincoln, a Massachusetts farmer who had started out in the militia and had worked his way up to major general. Lincoln had suffered the humiliation of surrendering Charles Town to the British. This was sweet revenge. Lincoln pointed to the field where the soldiers would lay down their guns.

Every allied face beamed with satisfaction and joy.

The British soldiers were exhausted and humiliated. One of the best armies in the world was surrendering to its mortal enemy— the French—and to a bunch of Americans "clad in small jackets of white cloth, dirty and ragged, and a number of them were almost barefoot," recorded Baron von Closen. Joseph Plumb Martin recalled, "The British paid the Americans little attention as they passed them, but they eyed the French with considerable malice depicted in their countenances."

The British turned their faces to the French line, to insult the Americans. Lafayette responded by ordering his regiment's fifes to strike up "Yankee Doodle," a popular American song. According to Major General Henry Lee, "the band's blare made them turn their eyes" to the Americans.

"The British officers in general behaved like boys who had been whipped at school. Some bit their lips; some pouted; others cried. Their round, broad-brimmed hats were well-adapted to the occasion, hiding those faces they were ashamed to show," recalled a New Jersey officer. At the order to "ground arms!" some of them threw down their weapons like angry children.

One Scottish soldier remembered that "the scene made a deep impression at the moment, for the mortification and unfeigned sorrow of the soldiers will never fade from my memory. Some cursed, some went so far as to shed tears, while one man, a corporal, who stood near me, embraced his firelock and then threw it on the ground, exclaiming, 'May you never get so good a master again!'" Stephan Popp, a Hessian soldier in the Ansbach Bayreuth Regiment, allied with the British army, recalled, "We were marched to a level plain, where the French Hussars formed a circle around us, and there we lay down our arms, etc. All the French and American generals were there . . . who showed great kindness to our men."

The following day, Cornwallis wrote to Clinton: "I have the mortification to inform your Excellency that I have been forced to give up the posts of York and Gloucester, and to surrender

Where was James? Unfortunately, the historical record does not tell us where James was during the surrender. One can imagine that he made sure to attend, since he had worked so hard toward this outcome, and records imply that he was at Lafayette's headquarters.

the troops under my command, by capitulation on the 19th instant as prisoners of war to the combined forces of America and France."

On the same day as the surrender, October 19, 1781, unknown to Cornwallis, an armada of Royal Navy ships and seven thousand reinforcements set sail from New York to rescue him.

This grand scene shows Yorktown from the French perspective. It is a copy of a painting of the surrender by a French artist originally painted for King Louis XVI in 1786. This copy was owned by Rochambeau. Notice that the foreground is filled with a variety of spectators.

CHAPTER

22

FREEDOM'S LONG ROAD

To the thousands gathered that day to witness the surrender, what did it all mean? Did they know they were watching a great moment in world history? They couldn't know that across the Atlantic, the first domino in a chain had begun falling. The British public quickly lost interest in supporting the war. Yorktown was the last great clash between the allied and British armies.

Many people, white and black, sacrificed their lives fighting for the cause of liberty. All the talk of freedom and equality during the American Revolution began to make more people think: If all men were created equal, as the Declaration of Independence stated, and liberty was a God-given right, then how was slavery just? A year before Yorktown, the Pennsylvania legislature made history by passing an Act for the Gradual Abolition of Slavery, the first law ending slavery adopted by a democracy. Three years after that, in 1783, Massachusetts became the first state to abolish slavery immediately. In the years to come, other Northern states, with economies less reliant on agriculture and less tied to the system of slavery, would follow those examples.

But for many enslaved people, freedom was a long time coming. An enslaved poet named Jupiter Hamon summed up the dashed high hopes of enslaved people at the end of the war: "That liberty is a great thing we know from our own feelings, and we may likewise judge so from the conduct of the white people in the late war. How much money has been spent and how many lives have been lost to defend their liberty! I must say that I have hoped that God would open their eyes, when they were so much engaged for liberty, to think of the state of the poor blacks, and to pity us."

James, still enslaved, returned to serving William Armistead. In May 1782, seven months after Yorktown, the Virginia General Assembly passed a law allowing slave owners to emancipate their slaves. Five months later, the legislature passed a law freeing a small number of enslaved men who had served in the military in place of their owners. But the law did not include those who had served as spies. No evidence indicates that William Armistead made any movement to free James. However, slaves themselves could also apply to the General Assembly for freedom based on meritorious service (something commendable that they had done). James wrote a petition, which he submitted to the legislature, and with it, a letter of support from Lafayette. The letter read:

> This is to certify that the bearer by the name
> of James has done essential services to me
> while I had the honor to command in this
> state. His intelligences from the enemy's camp
> were industriously collected and faithfully
> delivered. He perfectly acquitted himself with
> some important commissions I gave him and
> appears to me entitled to every reward his
> situation can admit of. Nov 21, 1784

James's efforts paid off. While it took time to get the legislature's attention, finally, on January 9, 1787, the Speaker of the

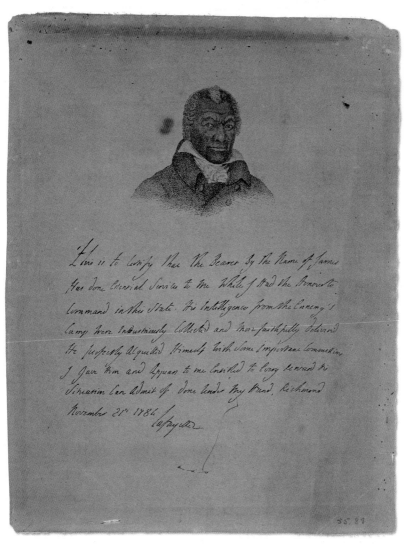

Around the time of Lafayette's triumphant tour of America in 1826, artist John Blennerhasset Martin sold souvenir handbills (printed pages) that bore James Lafayette's likeness above a facsimile of the Lafayette certificate.

The October 29, 1824, *Richmond Enquirer* reported the reunion between Lafayette and James.

House signed a bill that stated: "Be it there enacted, that the said James, from and after the passing of this act, enjoy as full freedom as if he had been born free."

Five years after Yorktown and after the enslaved men who had served as soldiers in the military were free, James too was free!

In the end, his trust in Lafayette had paid off. In gratitude, James chose the surname Lafayette. He would be known for the rest of his life as James Lafayette.

In 1824, Americans were excited by the news that the sixty-seven-year-old General Lafayette, the last living French general of the American Revolution, was planning a tour of the United States to celebrate the nation's fiftieth birthday. During his two-day visit to the Yorktown battlefield, thousands of well-wishers turned out to glimpse him. A *Richmond-Enquirer* article reported what happened: "A black man, even, who had rendered him service by way of information as a spy, for which he was liberated by the state, was recognized by Lafayette in the crowd, called to him by name, and taken into his embrace."

✶ EPILOGUE ✶

THE REST OF THE STORY

After the Siege of Yorktown, Washington immediately asked de Grasse if the French navy would support an attempt to liberate the cities of Charles Town and Savannah. The admiral's disappointing answer was no, the navy was needed back in the West Indies. The French navy departed, and Washington's forces split: Some went south to join General Nathanael Greene, and others went back to New York. Rochambeau's army stayed behind to guard Yorktown. They spent the winter in the Williamsburg area and returned north the following summer.

News of the victory reached Philadelphia in the early hours of October 24. Bells began pealing, waking residents from their sleep. People flocked to churches to thank God, fireworks displays lit up the skies, and cannons boomed in triumph.

In Yorktown, Rochambeau quickly dispatched two ships to take the news to the king in France. If something happened to one ship, he hoped, the other would arrive. One narrowly escaped capture by British warships. King Louis XVI was thrilled to hear the news and ordered a celebration across France.

It took almost five weeks for the news to reach London. Upon opening Clinton's message, Prime Minister Lord North reportedly said, "Oh God! It is all over." King George III, however, was not ready to give up the fight.

WAR'S END

After Yorktown, roughly thirty thousand British soldiers remained on American soil, occupying three major cities: New York, Charles Town,

and Savannah. General Washington did not know if the British would launch a new military campaign the following spring. But the winds of public opinion shifted, and the British public lost the will to continue the fight. In February 1782, Britain's Parliament passed a bill authorizing the king to make peace with America. In February the following year, 1783, King George III issued a proclamation notifying the world that the war was over.

Finally, seven months later, in September 1783, Great Britain signed the Treaty of Paris, which acknowledged the United States to be "free, sovereign [ruling themselves] and independent states."

GENERAL SIR HENRY CLINTON

Five months after Yorktown, General Clinton's superiors ordered him back to Britain. He returned in disgrace, receiving much of the blame for the failure in Virginia. He fought public perception and tried to shift blame to Cornwallis. Clinton eventually won a seat in Parliament, earned a rank of full general, and briefly served as governor of Gibraltar, where he died in 1795.

GENERAL LORD CHARLES CORNWALLIS

After the surrender, a few members of Congress wanted General Cornwallis executed immediately for war crimes committed by his army in the South. Under the terms of the surrender, though, he was permitted to leave for British headquarters in New York City.

Cornwallis enjoyed the most successful postwar career of all the British military leaders in America. Despite his embarrassing defeat at

Yorktown, he returned to Britain a hero and remained on good terms with the king. The British government published a report favorable to Cornwallis and unfavorable to Clinton. In 1786, the king made him a prestigious Knight of the Garter and appointed him commander in chief of British forces in India.

He served two terms in India, where he died in 1805 at age sixty-seven. The House of Commons voted that a memorial and statue to his memory be erected in St. Paul's Cathedral, London.

BENEDICT ARNOLD

After he left Virginia in May 1781, Arnold returned to New York City and convinced General Clinton to allow him to take a force to raid the port of New London, Connecticut, near where he grew up. His troops burned much of the town to the ground, then captured Fort Griswold and slaughtered American militiamen guarding it. He requested to go to Britain and took his family there in December 1781, traveling on the same ship as Cornwallis. Even in Britain, his reputation had been damaged by his betrayal of his country. Few people trusted him. He advocated for continuing the war and requested to return to New York. Leadership denied the request. After the war, he spent time in Canada but died in London and was buried there. Today, his name is synonymous with "traitor."

ENSLAVED VIRGINIANS

Historians estimate that at least 500 enslaved Virginians earned their freedom by serving in a military capacity during the war, many as substitutes for their owners. The Virginia General Assembly awarded them freedom in 1782. Of the roughly 6,000 enslaved Virginians who escaped to the British, only 2,000 managed to leave New York with the last British forces and resettle free in the British colony of Nova Scotia. The others either perished of disease or were forced to return to their owners.

The number of enslaved people in Virginia continued to grow with new births. It went from 210,000 at war's start to 236,000 by war's end. For the most part, laws regulating slavery became stricter after the war. However, in 1782 the Virginia legislature passed a law allowing slave owners to free their slaves, and the free black population grew from 2,000 in 1782 to 20,000 in 1800. However, free blacks had many restrictions: They couldn't vote, join the militia, or serve on a jury, and they were required to carry papers with them wherever they traveled.

GENERAL GEORGE WASHINGTON

At the close of the war, George Washington said farewell to his officers and resigned from the military, never again expecting to wear his uniform. He returned to his beloved Mount Vernon and would have been content with private life, but he agreed to serve as president of a convention of delegates that gathered in 1787 to discuss ways to improve governance of the new nation. The meeting's attendees, all white men, decided to write a new constitution for the United States and once again turned to Washington. The Constitution called for an American President and he was the perfect man for the job. Elected unanimously, George Washington was sworn in as the first president of the United States in April 1789. After serving for eight years, he declined to run for a third term and returned to private life. He died suddenly at Mount Vernon in December 1799. His will specified that his 123 enslaved workers should be freed on the death of his wife, Martha. This did not include the 153 enslaved people she owned.

FRANCE

The notions of freedom that swirled in the American air blew across the Atlantic Ocean and into France. They helped influence a period of social and political upheaval called the French Revolution, which ended the monarchy. King Louis XVI and his wife, Marie Antoinette, who had supported the American war for independence against King George III, were executed along with many other French nobles.

The new French Republic and the United States became allies, and the two nations fought together in two world wars and other conflicts. America was able to pay back a debt of gratitude in 1944 when its military helped to liberate occupied France from the Nazis.

GENERAL LAFAYETTE

Upon Lafayette's return to France in December 1781, King Louis XVI made him a brigadier general. Lafayette never asked the United States to reimburse him for his own expenses that he had spent to support the American Revolution. He became one of the most popular people in France and proved invaluable to the Americans negotiating the peace treaty to end the war. His association with the monarchy, however, landed him in prison for five years during the French Revolution. President George Washington tried to free him but had no power to do so. Lafayette lost his fortune during the upheaval, and several times the US Congress voted to give him financial gifts. Ten years after Lafayette's triumphant return tour to the United States in 1824–25, he died. America sent soil from Bunker Hill, near Boston, a battlefield site of the American Revolution, to cover his grave in Paris. More than ninety cities, townships, and counties in the United States are named for him.

GENERAL ROCHAMBEAU

Rochambeau returned to France in early 1783. King Louis XVI made him a prestigious Marshal of France for distinguished military achievement. During the French Revolution, his close connections with the monarchy landed him in prison for six months, and he was almost executed. With the birth of the French Republic, the new leader, Napoleon Bonaparte, presented him with the new Legion of Honor, the republic's most prestigious award. He spent his last years working on a memoir and died peacefully at his home in the country in 1807.

JAMES LAFAYETTE

As with Lafayette's life before freedom, few historical sources exist to reveal much about his later life. He took a job at a gristmill and purchased forty acres in New Kent County. At some point, he encountered an artist, John Blennerhasset Martin, in Richmond who became fascinated with his story. The only known portrait of Lafayette, painted by Martin, resides in the collection of the Valentine Museum in Richmond.

Little is known of Lafayette's family: his wife, Sylvia, and several children. He eventually earned enough money to buy them from their masters. For a time before his children reached the minimum age by law when they could be freed, they were legally considered his slaves. Finally, when they reached the required age, he officially manumitted (freed) them. In 1792, the Virginia General Assembly passed a law requiring all free blacks such as Lafayette to register with their local officials and receive a certificate of freedom that they were required to carry at all times. The freedom he achieved would never look the same as that of a white person.

In 1818, Lafayette applied to Virginia for a pension as a military veteran and was granted one annually for the rest of his life. Lafayette died at age eighty-two, either at home in New Kent County, Virginia, or in Baltimore; the sources disagree. He may have been in Baltimore visiting one of his children who had been forced to move out of state due to changing Virginia laws.

YORKTOWN

On October 20, the day after the surrender, Baron von Closen wrote in his journal, "I will never forget how frightful and disturbing was the appearance of the city of York, from the fortifications on the crest to the strand below . . . Most of the houses were riddled by cannon fire, and there were almost no window-panes in the houses." Of the more than two hundred buildings, fewer than seventy remained in Yorktown after the siege. In 1782, a year after the battle, young Mildred Smith wrote to her friend Betsy, who had fled the British with her family the year before. Smith had moved back to the family home in Yorktown, where the girls had grown up. "Were you to be suddenly and unexpectedly set down in the very spot where you and I have so often played together—in that very garden where we gathered flowers or stole your father's choice fruit—you would not recognize a solitary vestige of what it once was . . . it is shocking!"

Today, Yorktown is a quiet riverside village, restored to its eighteenth-century appearance. The preserved battlefield is owned by the American people and interpreted by the National Park Service. The state of Virginia runs a museum that also tells the story. A large eighty-four-foot-high column topped by "Lady Liberty," called the Yorktown Victory Monument, dominates the landscape, standing on a bluff overlooking the beach. The Continental Congress commissioned it shortly after the battle, though it took more than a hundred years to get built.

★ PLACES TO VISIT ★

HISTORY COMES ALIVE WHEN YOU VISIT THE PLACES where it happened. Many sites connected to this sweeping story have been preserved and are open to the public.

YORKTOWN BATTLEFIELD—The National Park Service maintains the site, including traces of the original siege lines, the surrender field, the Nelson house, the Moore house, and remains of redoubts 9 and 10.

AMERICAN REVOLUTION MUSEUM AT YORKTOWN—Owned and run by the state of Virginia, the museum features long- and short-term exhibitions about the siege, as well as an outdoor farm site and military encampment with cannon demonstrations and other presentations.

MOUNT VERNON—George and Martha Washington's estate includes their home, outbuildings, gardens, animals, and their graves, as well as reproduction slave quarters and a cemetery of enslaved workers.

VALENTINE MUSEUM—This Richmond museum owns the only known life portrait of James Lafayette.

NEW KENT COUNTY COURTHOUSE, NEW KENT, VIRGINIA—A state historical marker tells James Lafayette's story.

WASHINGTON-ROCHAMBEAU HISTORIC TRAIL—The route is maintained by the National Park Service and includes 680 miles of land and water trails and hundreds of historic sites in nine states. See w3r-us .org/site-category/historic-site.

JOSEPH WEBB HOUSE, OLD WETHERSFIELD, CONNECTICUT —Site of the May 1781 meeting between Rochambeau and Washington.

NEWPORT, RHODE ISLAND—A statue of Rochambeau stands on the waterfront and numerous houses that lodged French officers have been preserved, including the William Vernon House, Rochambeau's headquarters and the site of meetings with George Washington.

MONTICELLO—Thomas Jefferson's home is preserved. You can drive up the mountain and imagine Jefferson fleeing down it.

⋆ TIMELINE ⋆

1775

> **APRIL 19**—Lexington and Concord, first battles in the war for American independence

> **JUNE 15**—Congress makes George Washington commander in chief of Continental Army

1776

> **JULY 4**—Final text of "Declaration of Independence" approved

> **JULY 5**—Patrick Henry becomes Virginia's first state governor

> **SEPTEMBER 15**—British occupy New York City

> **DECEMBER 26**—Governor Henry issues a proclamation calling on Virginians to join the militia

1777

> **JULY 31**—Congress commissions the Marquis de Lafayette a major general

> **AUGUST 5**—Washington and Lafayette meet for the first time

> **OCTOBER 17**—General John Burgoyne surrenders at Saratoga, leading to a French alliance

1778

> **FEBRUARY 6**—US and France sign French Alliance

1779

> **JUNE 1**—Thomas Jefferson becomes second governor of Virginia

1780

    APRIL 27—Lafayette returns to America

    JULY 10/11—French troops arrive at Newport, RI

    SEPTEMBER 21—Washington and the comte de Rochambeau meet for the first time, in Hartford, CT

    SEPTEMBER 24—Benedict Arnold defects to the British

    DECEMBER 30—Arnold leads a British force into Virginia

1781

    MARCH 6—Washington meets with Rochambeau in Newport

    MARCH 16—First Battle of the Capes

    MARCH 27—General William Phillips arrives in Portsmouth, VA

    MAY 13—Phillips dies

    MAY 15—Governor Jefferson and General Assembly flee Richmond toward Charlottesville

    MAY 20—General Lord Charles Cornwallis arrives in Virginia

    MAY 21/22—Washington meets with Rochambeau in Wethersfield, CT

    JUNE 1—Arnold leaves Virginia, travels back to New York City

    JUNE 4—Colonel Banastre Tarleton raids Charlottesville, capturing several legislators and almost capturing Jefferson at Monticello

JUNE 10—French army begins march from Newport to New York

JULY 4–6—Cornwallis plans to move army across the James River; Battle of Green Spring

JULY 6—French army arrives at encampment in Philipsburg, New York

JULY 7—Cornwallis arrives at Portsmouth

AUGUST 1–2—Cornwallis and army encamp at Yorktown and across York River at Gloucester Point

AUGUST 14—Washington and Rochambeau receive word that the comte de Grasse is taking his French fleet to the Chesapeake

AUGUST 17—Washington writes de Grasse that they are committed to Virginia

AUGUST 19—Rochambeau and Washington break camp in New York: 2,500 Americans, 4,000 French

AUGUST 31—Rochambeau and Washington in Philadelphia

SEPTEMBER 5—Second Battle of the Capes

SEPTEMBER 14—Rochambeau and Washington arrive in Williamsburg

SEPTEMBER 17—Cornwallis learns that the British navy was repulsed and is going back to New York

SEPTEMBER 17—Washington visits de Grasse on his flagship

SEPTEMBER 26—American and French armies reunite in Williamsburg

SEPTEMBER 28—Entire combined army marches from Williamsburg to Yorktown

OCTOBER 5–6—Digging begins on the first line of trenches

OCTOBER 9—First siege line complete; big guns begin barrage

OCTOBER 11—Second siege line begins

OCTOBER 14—Allies storm redoubts 9 and 10

OCTOBER 16–17—(Early hours) Cornwallis attempts evacuation to Gloucester, fails due to storm

OCTOBER 17—Cornwallis asks for cease-fire

OCTOBER 19—British surrender at Yorktown

OCTOBER 24—News of surrender reaches Congress in Philadelphia

NOVEMBER 19—News of surrender arrives at Versailles; French king and queen overjoyed

NOVEMBER 25—Prime Minister Lord North learns of British surrender

1783

SEPTEMBER 3—Treaty of Paris is signed, ending the American war for independence

✷ AUTHOR'S NOTE ✷

OF THE BOOK'S MAIN CHARACTERS, JAMES LAFAYETTE is most mysterious because of his espionage activity and his status as an enslaved person for much of his life. Spies and slaves did not leave much evidence behind. The two main sources of information about him are his applications for manumission and for a pension. While a variety of information has been written about him over the years, I have tried to include only what can be documented by solid evidence. In some rare cases, I have guessed how he might have acted based on the options available to him. Among the big holes in his story are: (1) When did James begin his service with Lafayette? (2) Where was James during the Siege of Yorktown and the surrender? (3) What was the nature of his work with General Cornwallis? One story describes Cornwallis's shock upon seeing James in Lafayette's tent after the surrender when Lafayette was hosting British leadership, per military custom. Supposedly, at that point Cornwallis realized James was a double agent. I decided not to include this story because its source is questionable. Visitors to New Kent Courthouse in Virginia today can see a historical marker dedicated to James.

The relationship between Generals Clinton and Cornwallis is fascinating. After the war, they reported different interpretations of what had happened. Clinton claimed that Cornwallis had disobeyed his orders when he marched into Virginia. Conversely, Cornwallis said he had not heard from Clinton and needed to make timely decisions without specific instruction.

Astute readers who have read my book *Star-Spangled* may notice a link with this story. Major Charles Cochrane, who delivered an important message to Cornwallis at Yorktown and unfortunately died in a particularly gruesome fashion, was the brother of Admiral Alexander Cochrane, a main character in *Star-Spangled*. This incident at Yorktown is mentioned in that book.

Finally, should the military effort at Yorktown be identified as the Battle of Yorktown or the Siege of Yorktown? Though it is often referred to as a battle, siege is more accurate. The armies did not meet on a field of battle at Yorktown.

✶ GLOSSARY ✶

armada—a fleet of warships

artillery—projectile-firing weapons including field guns, such as cannons, howitzers, and mortars, which were lighter in weight and easier to move; and siege guns, which were heavy, generally stayed in place, and were designed to bombard fortifications and cities

battery—a collection of artillery; a fortification equipped with artillery

campaign—military operations aimed at a specific objective

cannon—a large gun for firing heavy projectiles

Continental Army—military unit made up of trained soldiers from around the thirteen colonies who enlisted for a set term and were (sometimes) paid by Congress and led by experienced soldiers

dragoon—a member of the British cavalry

earthwork—a barrier of soil created for use as a fortification

flagship—the ship carrying the admiral, the top commander

forage—to go in search of provisions; food for horses or cattle

fusilier—a member of a British army regiment

Great Britain—a country that included England, Scotland, and Wales.

Hessian—a mercenary, or paid-for-hire, soldier used by the British and native to several German-speaking areas, including the state of Hesse

howitzer—a short cannon for firing balls and shells

light infantry / light dragoons—certain type of foot soldiers carrying lighter equipment and easily mobile

line of march—the route taken by a column of troops

marquis—a title designating a specific rank of nobility in France

militia—citizen soldiers who may train but are not full-time soldiers

mortar—a short gun for firing bombs

paymaster—person in the military authorized to pay wages

quartermaster—officer in the military charged with providing clothing, fuel, transportation, and lodging

reconnaissance—an exploratory military observation of enemy territory

redcoat—common name for British infantry soldiers due to their red uniform

redoubt—an enclosed earthwork built to defend a prominent point

republican—a form of government where the power comes from the citizens who vote and elect representatives

ship of the line (also called line of battle ship)—a type of naval warship constructed between the seventeenth and nineteenth centuries to take part in a naval tactic known as line of battle, in which two columns of opposing warships would maneuver to bring the greatest gun power against the enemy.

tattoo—a signal beat on a drum telling soldiers to go to their quarters

topsail—the second sail up a mast, counting from the bottom

transport—a boat used to transport troops

⋆ NOTES ⋆

INTRODUCTION

xiix   "I beg it": Ellis, 70.

xv   "That these United": United States Declaration of Independence.

CHAPTER 1: A New Major General

2   "The distress I": Unger, 33.

2   "These men have": Ibid.

2   "a young nobleman": Ibid., 33–34.

2   "four days later": Ibid., 35.

3   "The farther I": Lafayette, *Memoirs, 1:42.*

3   "When I felt": Ibid., 1:13.

4   "After the sacrifices": Ibid., 1:17.

4   "Whereas the Marquis": Unger, 38.

5   "tales of war": Ibid., 3.

6   "I could not": Lafayette, *Memoirs,* 1:10.

7   "A youth of": Ibid., 1:13–14.

8   "It is certain": Unger, 26–27.

8   "zeal and sacrifice": Lafayette, *Memoirs,* 1:16.

9   "could not promise": Unger, 40.

9   "I wish to": Ibid.

CHAPTER 2: Autumn of Disappointment

11   "It is to": Lafayette, *Memoirs, 1:19.*

13   "illustrious and important": Ketchum, 32.

15   "Last week arrived": Abigail Adams to John Adams, May 1, 1780, *Adams Family Papers: An Electronic Archive,* Massachusetts Historical Society. See www.masshist.org/digitaladams.

15   "We are now": Ferreiro, 219.

15   "I have the": Washington to Rochambeau, July 16, 1780, Founders Online. See founders.archives.gov/documents/Washington/99-01-02-02521.

17   "Permit me to": Lafayette, *Memoirs,* 1:125–26.

CHAPTER 3: First Meeting

23 "He is very": Lauberdière, 70.

23 "His dignified address" "His face is": Ketchum, 43–44.

24 "He looks like": Ketchum, 43–44.

25 "We could only": Ketchum, 45.

CHAPTER 4: A Traitor Exposed

29 "There has been": Chernow, 141.

29 "I cannot describe": Unger, 124.

29 "By a lucky": Washington to Rochambeau, September 26, 1780, Founders Online. See founders.archives.gov/documents/Washington/99-01-02-03401.

30 "I know not": Ketchum, 79.

CHAPTER 5: Plundering Virginia

34 "This moment Commodore": Kranish, 166.

37 "he would not": Ewald, 261.

37 "would hang him": Ibid.

39 "the most delightful": Kranish, 14.

39 "I wish well": Ibid., 184.

40 "Where is the": Ibid., 193.

41 "It seemed like": Ibid.

41 "terrible things happened": Ibid., 195.

41 "many explosions [that]": Ibid., 194.

44 "As Mr. Jefferson": Ibid., 195.

44 "private property was": Ibid.

44 "infamous beasts": Ketchum, 97.

44 "All the letters": Closen, 56.

45 "You are to": Unger, 131.

45 "I had returned": Ibid., 121.

46 "reveal to the": Kranish, 216.

46 "What should be": Ibid., 215.

46 "They will cut": Ibid.

CHAPTER 6: Happy Birthday, General

49   "are the most civilized": Ferreiro, 221.

52   "Yesterday was Your": Vail, 89.

52   "The arrival of": Closen, March 6, 1781.

52   "all the pomp": Vail, 90.

58   "If Admiral Arbuthnot": Philbrick, 68.

58   "This however may": Ibid., 71.

59   "extreme pain": Ibid., 74.

59   "Instead of having": Vail, 95.

61   "the Americans are": Philbrick, 139.

CHAPTER 7: The Perfect Spy

64   "There is one": Allen, 146.

CHAPTER 8: Redcoats Equal Freedom

73   "gentlemen's houses . . . in": Thompson, 279.

73   "a large supply": Ibid.

73   "expressed his personal": Ibid.

76   "When the enemy": Ibid., 280.

76   "You will do": Ibid.

76   "It would have": Ibid.

77   "secretly wished that": Urwin, *When Freedom*, 13.

77   "It is said": Ibid.

78   "all the negroes": Ibid., 14.

78   "as to the": Ibid.

81   "The number or": Ibid., 15–16.

81   "Any place this": Ewald, 305.

81   "[Slaves] were given": Urwin, When Freedom, 14.

81   "the infatuation of": MacMaster and Honyman, May 11, 1781.

81   "enticed and flattered": Urwin, When Freedom, 14.

000   "had lost every": Maass, 99.

000   "No Negroes have": Urwin, *When Freedom*, 16.

CHAPTER 9: Clash of the Generals

88 "I am very": Carpenter, 214.

88 "Until Virginia is": Ibid.

88 "I should certainly": Maass, 18.

88 "My wonder at": Ibid.

88 "we have not": O'Shaughnessy, 220.

89 "This country [England]": Patterson, 194.

90 "I am now": Ibid.

CHAPTER 10: Jefferson on the Run

95 "Was I to": Patterson, 293.

95 "By seizing the": Maass, 55.

96 "to prevent the": Carpenter, 286.

96 "we have everything": Maass, 55.

96 "We are in": Ibid., 57.

96 "all the fine": Ibid., 67.

97 "carry the sword": Urwin, *When Freedom*, 10.

99 "All public stores": Ibid.

100 "range about the": Maass, 76.

100 "What an alarming": Kranish, 275.

100 "The nearer the": Ibid.

106 "Virginia is not": Maass, 119.

CHAPTER 11: Ways to Freedom

109 "Would it not": Kranish, 254.

110 "take measures immediately": See encyclopediavirginia.org/entries
      /journals-of-the-continental-congress-march-29-1779.

112 "while there remain": Quarles, 64.

CHAPTER 12: Marching to New York

117 "The entire country": Lauberdière, 106.

120 "A finer body": Vail, 125–26.

121 "We now greet": Ibid., 137.

122 "General Washington's demonstration": Lauberdière, 104.

122 "his Excellency the": Vail, 130.

122 "our troops . . . appeared": Ibid.

122 "I had a": Ibid.

122 "In beholding this": Ibid., 135.

CHAPTER 13: The Town of York

125 "the passage of": O'Shaughnessy, 278.

125 "the boy": Maass, 74.

126 "This devil Cornwallis": Ibid., 139.

129 "They would inevitably": Urban, 262.

129 "It is shocking": Urwin, *When Freedom*, 19.

130 "a very pretty": Hatch, 50.

CHAPTER 14: Decision at Last

135 "A correspondent of": Lafayette, *Letters*.

137 "The capture of": Nagy, *Invisible*, 214.

137 "An attempt on": Ibid..

140 "I could scarce": Vail, 145.

140 "I shall be": Ibid.

142 "I then suggested": Ibid., 118.

142 "Should a [French]": Philbrick, 151.

143 "by being upon": Ibid., 152.

143 "as clear to": Ibid.

143 "We have determined": Vail, 177.

143 "I hope you": Philbrick, 178.

145 "The enemy have": Founders Online. See founders.archives.gov
/documents/Washington/99-01-02-06792.

CHAPTER 15: The Big Secret

148 "much trouble was": Nagy, *Invisible*, 223.

148 "Our destination has": Ibid., 224.

149 "French bakery to": Ibid., 225.

149 "But to assure": Lauberdière, 124.

149 "French ovens are": Nagy, *Invisible*, 225.

150 "Contracts are made": Ibid..

150 "Calculating people [and]": Lauberdière, 124.

151 "I have delayed": Nagy, *Invisible*, 229.

154 "Yesterday, at one": Moore, 475.

155 "After dinner, some": Ibid., 528.

155 "were absolutely amazed": Vail, 188.

156 "Mr. Clinton believed": Lauberdière, 133–34.

156 "the present time": Philbrick, 164.

156 "I am almost": Ibid., 169.

157 "waving his hat": Vail, 191.

157 "I never saw": Ibid.

157 "Long live Louis": Philbrick, 171.

157 "The General calls": Vail, 193.

157 "From this moment": Lauberdière, 145.

158 "One must not": Philbrick, 307.

CHAPTER 16: Battle at Sea

166 "upon this state": Philbrick, 196.

168 "An elegant seat": Ketchum, 182.

169 "the Marquis, riding": Vail, 202.

169 "embark[ed] on all": Ibid., 203.

170 "I take particular": Philbrick, 196.

174 "The most noble": Ibid., 199.

174 "Mon cher petit": Vail, 228.

175 "I am happy": Ibid., 229.

CHAPTER 17: Cornwallis Digs In

177 "For six weeks": Urban, 263.

180 "By intelligence which": Philbrick, 169.

180 "My provisions will": Ibid., 200.

180 "This place is": Ibid.

182 "a bold and": Ibid., 138.

182 "In the dark": Ibid., 201.

183 "It passed, however": Ibid.

183 "It is time": Ibid.

183 "I cannot conceal": Ibid., 202.

184 "I can testify": Greene, 92.

185 "The Commander in": Ibid., 111.

CHAPTER 18: The Siege Begins

189 "Your letter . . . has": Greene, 116.

191 "I am at": Ibid., 130.

193 "The enemy endeavored": Ibid., 131.

196 "We had not": Ibid., 154.

197 "The soil was": Ibid., 163.

197 "The work was": Ibid., 165.

197 "All were upon": Ketchum, 227.

197 "Everything is in": Greene, 70.

200 "I could hear": Ketchum, 227.

200 "This day, this": Ibid.

200 "Happy day! Forty-one": Greene, 192.

CHAPTER 19: A Ferocious Pounding

199 "shot and shells": Greene, 195.

201 "a number of": Ibid.

201 "[The bombs] are": Ibid., 201.

201 "sometimes burying itself": Ibid., 202.

203 "I am doing": Hallahan, 181.

203 "Nothing but a": Ibid..

204 "Anxious to see": Ketchum, 235.

204 "We anticipate the": Ellis, 135.

205 "The ships were": Greene, 210.

205 "Never could a": Ibid.

208 "I never saw": Ibid., 212.

208 "The heavy fire": Ferreiro, 269.

208 "The entire night": Hallahan, 181.

208 "I saw bombs": Döhla, 168–69.

209 "By their conduct": Greene, 223.

CHAPTER 20: Storming the Redoubts

211 "Nou verrons demain": Vail, 251.

211 "Never did greater": Greene, 225.

212 "We have it!": Chernow, 163.

214 "The Sappers and": Martin diary, 169. See books.google.com
    /books?id=ZbdcAAAAcAAJ&printsec=frontcover&source=gbs_ge
    _summary_r&cad=0#v=onepage&q&f=false.

214 "We had not": Ibid., 170.

218 "the Commander in": Greene, 256.

218 "This action, though": Ibid., 264.

220 "It was as": Philbrick, 226.

220 "Thus expired the": Greene, 277.

CHAPTER 21: A Deafening Quiet

223 "The whole peninsula": Philbrick, 226.

223 "I thought I": Denny, 44.

223 "wanton and inhuman": Philbrick, 227.

224 "Sir, I propose": Ketchum, 240.

224 "A solemn stillness": Ibid., 242.

225 "As soon as": Ibid.

226 "Lord Cornwallis cannot": Greene, 290.

230 "Every eye was": Ketchum, 249.

230 "You are mistaken": Ibid., 251.

231 "We are not": Greene, 294.

231 "clad in small": Ketchum, 252.

232 "The British paid": Martin diary, 174. See books.google.com
/books?id=ZbdcAAAAcAAJ&printsec=frontcover&source=gbs_ge
_s mmary_r&cad=0#v=onepage&q&f=false.

232 "the band's blare": Unger, 159.

232 "The British officers": Ketchum, 252.

232 "the scene made": Ibid., 253.

232 "We were marched": *The American Revolution: A World War*,
online exhibition, National Museum of American History. See
americanhistory.si.edu/american-revolution.

232 "I have the": Patterson, 329.

CHAPTER 22: Freedom's Long Road

237 "That liberty is": Quarles, 182.

238 "This is to": Legislative Petition for James, Slave Belonging to William
Armistead, 30 November 1786, box 179, folder 10, Library of
Virginia, Richmond.

241 "Be it there": Statutes of Virginia, William Waller Hening, ed., The
Statutes at Large: Being a Collection of All the Laws of Virginia,
from the First Session of the Legislature, in the Year 1619 . . .
(1809–1823), 12:380–381.271

241 "A black man": Salmon, 83. *Richmond Enquirer*, Volume 21, Number
52, 29 October 1824

EPILOGUE: The Rest of the Story

242 "Oh God": Hallahan, 249.

243 "free, sovereign[ruling]": Treaty of Paris, 1783; International Treaties
and Related Records, 1778-1974; General Records of the United
States Government, Record Group 11; National Archives.

248 "I will never": Closen, 155.

249 "Were you to": Ketchum, 270.

✴ BIBLIOGRAPHY ✴

Allen, Thomas B. *George Washington, Spymaster*. Washington, DC: National Geographic, 2004.

Carpenter, Stanley D. M. *Southern Gambit: Cornwallis and the British March to Yorktown*. Norman: University of Oklahoma Press, 2019.

Cecere, Michael. *The Invasion of Virginia, 1781*. Yardley, PA: Westholme, 2017.

———. *A Universal Appearance of War: The Revolutionary War in Virginia, 1775–1781*. Berwyn Heights, MD: Heritage Books, 2014.

Chernow, Ron. *Alexander Hamilton*. New York: Penguin, 2004.

Closen, Baron Ludwig von. *The Revolutionary Journal of Baron Ludwig von Closen, 1780–1783*. Translated and edited by Evelyn M. Acomb. Chapel Hill: Omohundro Institute and University of North Carolina Press, 2017.

Cook, Don. *The Long Fuse: How England Lost the American Colonies, 1760–1785*. New York: Atlantic Monthly, 1995.

Denny, Ebenezer. *Military Journal of Major Ebenezer Denny, an Officer in the Revolutionary and Indian Wars*. Philadelphia: J. B. Lippincott, for the Historical Society of Pennsylvania, 1859. See archive.org/details /militaryjournalo00denn/page/44/mode/2up.

Döhla, Johann Conrad. *A Hessian Diary of the American Revolution, by Johann Conrad Döhla*. Translated and edited by Brian Burgoyne. Norman: University of Oklahoma Press, 1990.

Ellis, Joseph J. *His Excellency George Washington*. New York: Vintage Books, 2004.

Ewald, Captain Johann. *Diary of the American War: A Hessian Journal*. Translated and edited by Joseph P. Tustin. New Haven, CT: Yale University Press, 1979.

Ferreiro, Larrie D. *Brothers at Arms: American Independence and the Men of France and Spain Who Saved It*. New York: Knopf, 2016.

Founders Online. National Archives and Records Administration. See founders.archives.gov.

Greene, Jerome. *The Guns of Independence: The Siege of Yorktown, 1781*. El Dorado Hills, CA: Savas Beatie, 2005.

Hallahan, William. *The Day the Revolution Ended, 19 October 1781*. Hoboken, NJ: John Wiley and Sons, 2004.

Hatch, Charles E., Jr. *"York under the Hill": Yorktown's Waterfront*. Historic Resource Study. Denver: Denver Service Center, National Park Service, 1973.

Journal of the American Revolution. allthingsliberty.com.

Ketchum, Richard M. *Victory at Yorktown: The Campaign That Won the Revolution*. New York: Henry Holt, 2004.

Kranish, Michael. *Flight from Monticello: Thomas Jefferson at War*. Oxford: Oxford University Press, 2010.

Lafayette, Marie-Joseph-Paul-Yves-Roch-Gilbert du Motier, Marquis de. *The Letters of Lafayette to Washington, 1777–1799*. Edited by Louis Gottschalk. Philadelphia: American Philosophical Society, 1976.

———. *Memoirs, Correspondence and Manuscripts of General Lafayette: Published by His Family*. Vol. 1, *American Revolution*. New York: Saunders and Otley, 1837. See books.google.bj /books?id=C0tBAAAAIAAJ&pg=PA3&hl=fr&source=gbs _toc_r&cad=3#v=onepage&q&f=false.

Lauberdière, Louis-François-Bertrand du Pont d'Aubevoye, comte de. *The Road to Yorktown: The French Campaigns in the American Revolution, 1780–1783*. Translated and annotated by Norman Desmarais. El Dorado Hills, California: Savas Beatie, 2021.

Legislative Petition for James, Slave Belonging to William Armistead, 30 November 1786. box 179, folder 10. Library of Virginia, Richmond.

Maass, John. *The Road to Yorktown: Jefferson, Lafayette, and the British Invasion of Virginia*. Charleston, SC: History Press, 2015.

MacMaster, Richard K., and Robert Honyman. "News of the Yorktown Campaign: The Journal of Dr. Robert Honyman, April 17–November 25, 1781." *Virginia Magazine of History and Biography 79*, no. 4 (October 1971): 387–426.

Martin, Joseph Plumb. *A Narrative of a Revolutionary Soldier*. New York: Signet Classics, 2010.

Moore, Frank, comp. *The Diary of the American Revolution*. Edited by John Anthony Scott. New York: Washington Square Press, 1967.

Nagy, John A. *George Washington's Secret Spy War: The Making of America's First Spymaster*. New York: St. Martin's Press, 2016.

———. *Invisible Ink: Spycraft of the American Revolution*. Yardley, PA: Westholme, 2010.

National Park Service National Washington-Rochambeau Revolutionary Route Association, Washington-Rochambeau National Historic Trail. See w3r-us.org.

Nelson, James. *George Washington's Great Gamble: And the Sea Battle That Won the American Revolution*. New York: McGraw-Hill, 2010.

O'Shaughnessy, Andrew Jackson. *The Men Who Lost America: British Leadership, the American Revolution, and the Fate of the Empire*. New Haven, CT: Yale University Press, 2013.

Patterson, Benton Rain. *Washington and Cornwallis: The Battle for America, 1775–1783*. Lanham, MD: Taylor, 2004.

Pearson, Michael. *Those Damned Rebels: The American Revolution as Seen through British Eyes*. Boston: Da Capo, 1972.

Philbrick, Nathaniel. *In the Hurricane's Eye: The Genius of George Washington and the Victory at Yorktown*. New York: Viking, 2018.

Quarles, Benjamin. *The Negro in the American Revolution*. New York: W. W. Norton, 1973.

Rees, John U. *They Were Good Soldiers: African Americans Serving in the Continental Army, 1775–1783*. Warwick, UK: Helion, 2019.

Rose, Alexander. *Washington's Spies: The Story of America's First Spy ring*. New York: Bantam Dell, 2006.

Salmon, John. "'A Mission of the Most Secret and Important Kind': James Lafayette and American Espionage in 1781." *Virginia Cavalcade* 31, no. 2 (Autumn 1981): 78–85.

Shachtman, Tom. *How the French Saved America*. New York: St. Martin's Press, 2017.

Shepherd, Samuel, comp. *The Statutes at Large of Virginia: From October Session 1792 to December Session 1806 [1807]*. 3 vols. 1835–36. Reprint, New York: AMS Press, 1970.

Taylor, Alan. *The Internal Enemy: Slavery and War in Virginia, 1772–1832*. New York: W. W. Norton, 2013.

Thompson, Mary. *The Only Unavoidable Subject of Regret: George Washington, Slavery, and the Enslaved Community at Mount Vernon*. Charlottesville: University of Virginia Press, 2019.

Unger, Harlow Giles. *Lafayette*. Hoboken, NJ: John Wiley and Sons, 2002.

Urban, Mark. *Fusiliers: The Saga of a British Redcoat Regiment in the American Revolution*. London: Walker Books, 2007.

Urwin, Gregory J. W. "'Abandoned to the Arts & Arms of the Enemy': Placing the 1781 Virginia Campaign in Its Racial and Political

Context." Harmon Memorial Lectures in Military History 57.
Colorado Springs, CO: United States Air Force Academy, 2014.
See usafa.edu/app/uploads/Harmon57.pdf.

————. "When Freedom Wore a Red Coat: How Cornwallis' 1781
Campaign Threatened the Revolution in Virginia." *Army History*, no.
68 (Summer 2008): 6–23.

Vail, Jini Jones. *Rochambeau: Washington's Ideal Lieutenant.* Tarentum, PA: Word
Association, 2011.

Willcox, William, ed. *The American Rebellion: Sir Henry Clinton's Narrative of His
Campaigns, 1775–1782,* New Haven, CT: Yale University Press, 1954.

Zall, Paul M. *Becoming American: Young People in the American Revolution.* North
Haven, CT: Linnet Books, 1993.

ACKNOWLEDGMENTS

MANY PEOPLE HELPED WITH THIS PROJECT AND DESERVE SPECIAL THANKS.

As a student in 1981, I traveled with my parents to the bicentennial program at Yorktown, where we listened to Presidents Ronald Reagan and François Mitterrand and watched hundreds of reenactors bring the surrender ceremony to life. That event fired my young imagination. I am thankful for parents who cultivated my love of the past by accommodating my history quests.

Years later, I first encountered James Lafayette's story in a magazine article and knew it had to be told. It took me a while to take on this story, mainly because James was such an elusive character, and I had to find solid documentation. My thanks to Kate Gruber at the Jamestown-Yorktown Foundation and LaVonne Allen at the New Kent County Historical Society for their generosity in sharing research. LaVonne's passion for James's story is inspiring. As character interpreters for the Colonial Williamsburg Foundation, Stephen Seals and Mark Schneider bring James Lafayette and the Marquis de Lafayette to life throughout the year. They, too, shared research and provided insight and suggestions along the way. If you want to "meet" James or Lafayette, find out when they are presenting a program and be sure to go, or find them online.

I'm indebted to staff at both the Jamestown-Yorktown Foundation (JYF), which runs the American Revolution Museum, and the Colonial National Historical Park, which preserves and interprets Yorktown battlefield. At JYF, my friends Pam Pettengell and Mark Howell offered both support and connections. Ed Ayres, historian and librarian at JYF, was a huge help in directing me to sources, answering many random questions, and reviewing the final manuscript. Robbie Smith, park ranger at Yorktown battlefield, went above and beyond when she started to give me a tour in the pouring rain, then kindly accommodated my schedule for a tour in the sunshine. She also reviewed the entire manuscript.

★ ACKNOWLEDGMENTS ★

I wish to thank the staff at the Virginia Room in the Fairfax County Library, Fairfax, Virginia. They manage an amazing collection and were always helpful.

Friends Conny and Dave Graft graciously hosted me during several research trips to Yorktown.

My thanks to Howard Morrison, my former colleague at the Smithsonian National Museum of American History, who showed me the Yorktown exhibit he developed and generously shared materials.

My first readers are dedicated and constructive and always offer excellent insight and improve my writing. Thank you to Mathina Calliope and Derek Baxter, Nancy and Larry Kuch, and Sandor Der—Sandor first suggested I write about spies in the American Revolution.

Final thanks go to the staff at Abrams Books, including my amazing editor, Howard Reeves, and the very capable Sara Sproull. I appreciate Howard's willingness to tackle tough history topics and always offer exacting insight. And to my agent, Alex Slater at the Trident Media Group, thank you for guiding me along my writing journey.

⭐ IMAGE CREDITS ⭐

✭ INDEX ✭